ROCK CHARTS
GUITAR 2000

The Biggest Hits, The Greatest Artists

Deluxe *Annual* Edition

Project Manager: Aaron Stang
Production Coordinator: Karl Bork
Art Layout and Design: Debbie Johns

CONTENTS

4 /ALL STAR
Smash Mouth

10 /AMERICAN BAD ASS
Kid Rock

26 /BACK TO SCHOOL
Deftones

32 /BAD RELIGION
Godsmack

330 /THE BAD TOUCH
Bloodhound Gang

21 /BREAK STUFF
Limp Bizkit

36 /CHANGE (IN THE HOUSE OF FLIES)
Deftones

40 /COWBOY
Kid Rock

334 /THE DOLPHIN'S CRY
Live

52 /DOWN
Stone Temple Pilots

76 /ENEMY
Days of the New

86 /EVERYTHING YOU WANT
Vertical Horizon

61 /EX-GIRLFRIEND
No Doubt

92 /FALLING AWAY FROM ME
Korn

102 /FALLS APART
Sugar Ray

97 /HEAVEN & HOT RODS
Stone Temple Pilots

108 /HEMORRHAGE
Fuel

117 /HOME
Staind

122 /I WALK ALONE
Oleander

129 /IN 2 DEEP
Kenny Wayne Shepherd Band

138 /KEEP AWAY
Godsmack

144 /KRYPTONITE
3 Doors Down

158 /LAST GOODBYE
Kenny Wayne Shepherd Band

168 /LOSER
3 Doors Down

153 /MAKE ME BAD
Korn

176 /MARIA MARIA
Santana

192 /MINORITY
Green Day

196 /MUDSHOVEL
Staind

210 /MY FAVORITE HEADACHE
Geddy Lee

201 /NO WAY OUT
Stone Temple Pilots

220 /NOOKIE
Limp Bizkit

226 /ONLY GOD KNOWS WHY
Kid Rock

234 /PUT YOUR LIGHTS ON
Santana

246 /REARRANGED
Limp Bizkit

270 /REVOLUTION IS MY NAME
Pantera

280 /RUN TO THE WATER
Live

288 /SIMPLE KIND OF LIFE
No Doubt

255 /SMOOTH
Santana

300 /SOMEBODY SOMEONE
Korn

305 /SOMEDAY
Sugar Ray

312 /SOUR GIRL
Stone Temple Pilots

318 /STUPIFY
Disturbed

325 /THEN THE MORNING COMES
Smash Mouth

344 /THEY STOOD UP FOR LOVE
Live

352 /TREMBLE FOR MY BELOVED
Collective Soul

358 /VOODOO
Godsmack

362 /WAS
Kenny Wayne Shepherd Band

375 /WASTING TIME
Kid Rock

382 /WEAPON AND THE WOUND
Days of the New

394 /YOU'RE A GOD
Vertical Horizon

ARTIST INDEX

3 DOORS DOWN
144 / Kryptonite
168 / Loser

BLOODHOUND GANG
330 / The Bad Touch

COLLECTIVE SOUL
352 / Tremble for My Beloved

DAYS OF THE NEW
76 / Enemy
382 / Weapon and the Wound

DEFTONES
26 / Back to School
36 / Change (In the House of Flies)

DISTURBED
318 / Stupify

FUEL
108 / Hemorrhage

GODSMACK
32 / Bad Religion
138 / Keep Away
358 / Voodoo

GREEN DAY
192 / Minority

**KENNY WAYNE
SHEPHERD BAND**
129 / In 2 Deep
158 / Last Goodbye
362 / Was

KID ROCK
10 / American Bad Ass
40 / Cowboy
226 / Only God Knows Why
375 / Wasting Time

KORN
92 / Falling Away From Me
153 / Make Me Bad
300 / Somebody Someone

GEDDY LEE
210 / My Favorite Headache

LIMP BIZKIT
21 / Break Stuff
220 / Nookie
246 / ReArranged

LIVE
334 / The Dolphin's Cry
280 / Run to the Water
344 / They Stood Up for Love

NO DOUBT
61 / Ex-Girlfriend
288 / Simple Kind of Life

OLEANDER
122 / I Walk Alone

PANTERA
270 / Revolution Is My Name

SANTANA
176 / Maria Maria
234 / Put Your Lights On
255 / Smooth

SMASH MOUTH
4 / All Star
325 / Then the Morning Comes

STAIND
117 / Home
196 / Mudshovel

STONE TEMPLE PILOTS
52 / Down
97 / Heaven & Hot Rods
201 / No Way Out
312 / Sour Girl

SUGAR RAY
102 / Falls Apart
305 / Someday

VERTICAL HORIZON
86 / Everything You Want
384 / You're a God

ALL STAR

Words and Music by
GREG CAMP

8

9

All Star – 6 – 6

AMERICAN BAD ASS

Words and Music by
R.J. "KID ROCK" RITCHIE,
JAMES HETFIELD and LARS ULRICH

All gtrs. w/dropped D tuning:
⑥=D

Moderate rock ♩ = 84

Are you   scared?

American Bad Ass - 11 - 1

Verse 1 & 2:

*Elec. Gtr. 1 simile 2nd time.

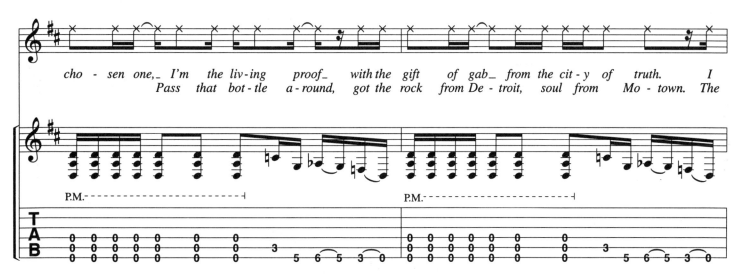

12

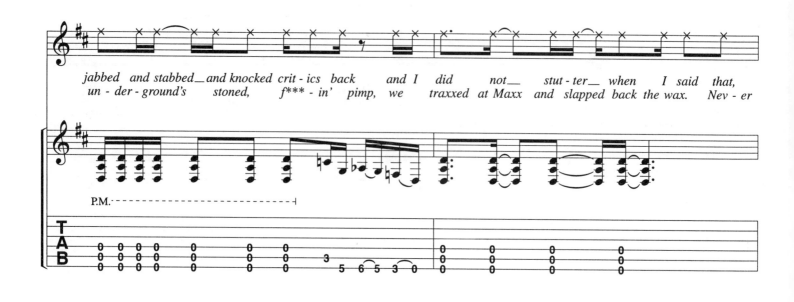

jabbed and stabbed__ and knocked crit - ics back and I did not__ stut - ter__ when I said that,
un - der - ground's stoned, f*** - in' pimp, we traxxed at Maxx and slapped back the wax. Nev - er

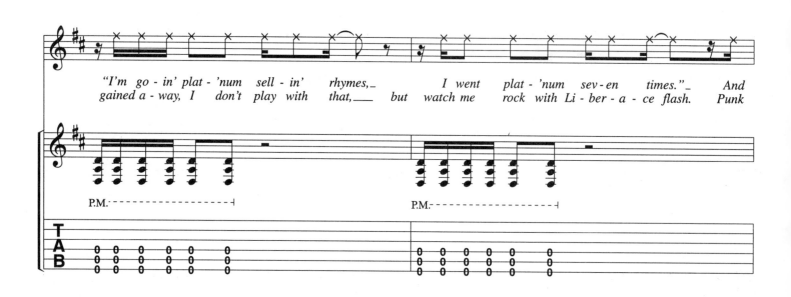

"I'm go - in' plat - 'num sell - in' rhymes,__ I went plat - 'num sev - en times."__ And
gained a - way, I don't play with that,__ but watch me rock with Li - ber - a - ce flash. Punk

still they're ill,__ they wan - na see us fry.__ I guess be - cause. that on - ly God knows why,
rock, the Clash,_ boy bands of trash._ I like John - ny Cash_ and Grand Mas - ter Flash,

Rhy. Fig. 2

14

16

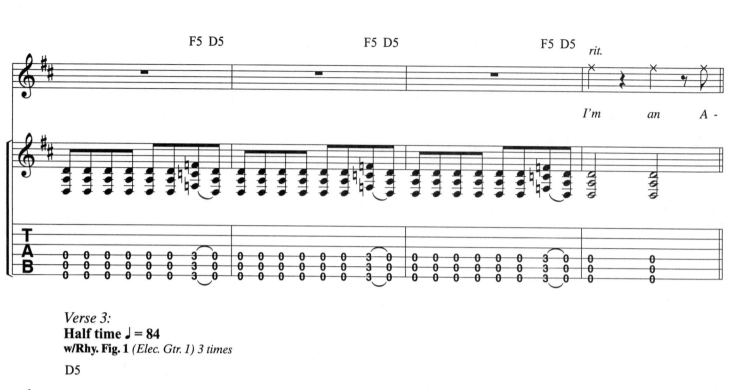

F5 D5   F5 D5   F5 D5   *rit.*

I'm   an   A-

Verse 3:
Half time ♩ = 84
w/Rhy. Fig. 1 *(Elec. Gtr. 1) 3 times*

D5

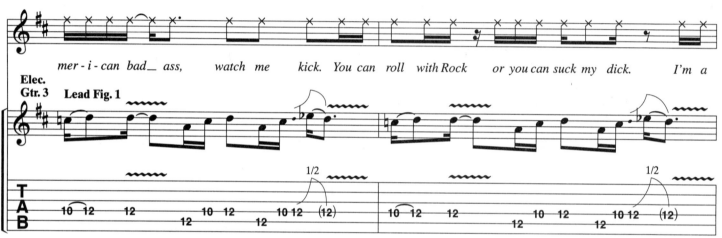

mer-i-can bad_ ass,   watch me   kick. You can roll with Rock   or you can suck my dick.   I'm a

Elec.
Gtr. 3   **Lead Fig. 1**

por-no   flick,   I'm like a-maz-ing grace,   I'm gon-na f*** some hos af-ter I rock this place.

end Lead Fig. 1

w/Lead Fig. 1 *(Elec. Gtr. 3) 3 times, simile*

Su-per Fly_ liv-in' dou-ble wide_ side, put on my glide_ so Joe C. can ride._ Full

American Bad Ass - 11 - 7

sacks to share_ bring-ing flash and flare. Got the long hair swing-in; mid-dle fin-ger in the air.

Snake skin suits, six-ty five Che-velle,_ see me ride in sin,_ hear the reb-el yell._ I won't

live to tell__ so, if you do, give the next gen-er-a-tion a big__ f*** you!_ Who

w/Rhy. Fig. 1 *(Elec. Gtr. 1) 1st 3 meas. only*

knew I'd grow a black punk wo-wo-ha. Said f*** high school,_ pissed on my di-plo-ma.

w/Rhy. Fig. 2 *(Elec. Gtr. 1)*

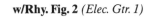

Smell the a-ro-ma, check my hitch._ I know it stinks in here_ 'cause I'm the s***, s***, s***, s***, s***.

Chorus:
w/Rhy. Fig. 3 *(Elec. Gtr. 1)*
D5

w/Fill 1 *(Elec. Gtr. 2)*

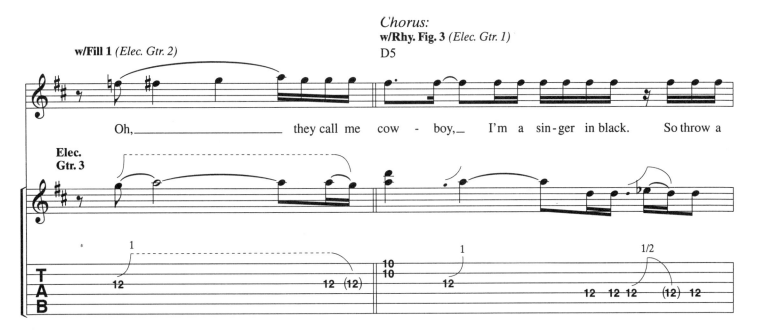

Oh,_____ they call me cow-boy,_ I'm a sin-ger in black. So throw a

fin-ger in the air, let me see where you're at. Say, "hey, hey." Let me hear where you're at. Say,

"Hey, hey." I'm giv-in' it back____ so say, "Hey, hey" *Show me some mad__ when you say,*

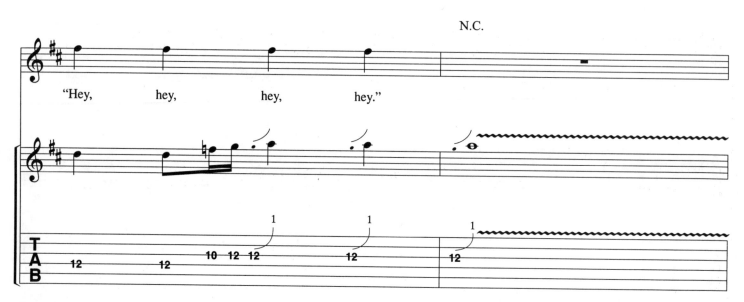

"Hey, hey, hey, hey."

w/Rhy. Fig. 3 *(Elec. Gtr.) meas. 5 & 6 only, 3 times*

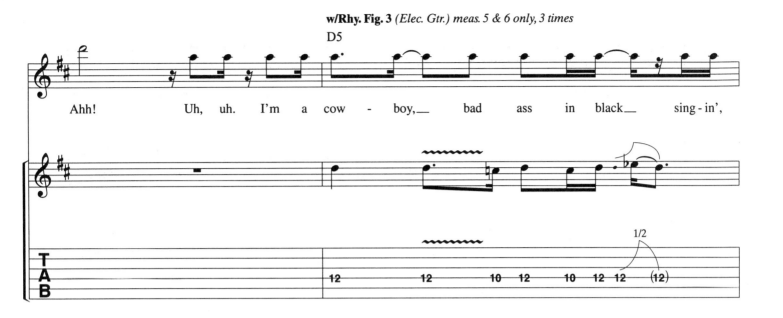

Ahh! Uh, uh. I'm a cow - boy,_ bad ass in black_ sing - in',

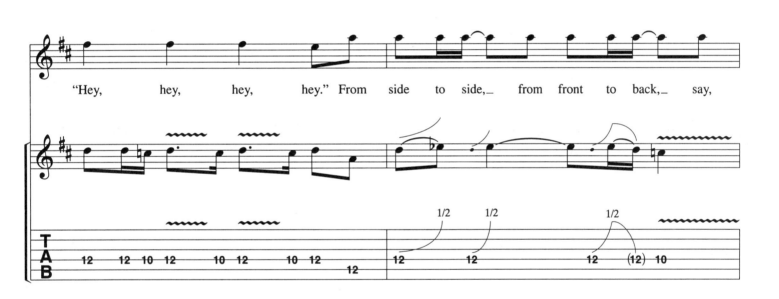

"Hey, hey, hey, hey." From side to side,_ from front to back,_ say,

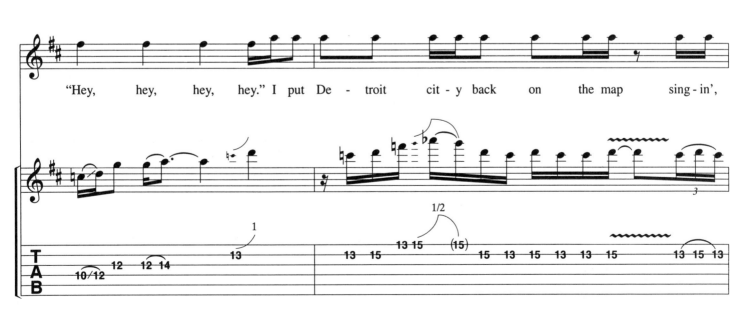

"Hey, hey, hey, hey." I put De - troit cit - y back on the map sing - in',

American Bad Ass - 11 - 10

"Hey, hey, hey, hey." Kid Rock's in the house and that's where I'm at!

BREAK STUFF

Lyrics by Fred Durst
Music by Wes Borland, Sam Rivers, John Otto,
Leor Dimant and Brendan O'Brien

†All gtrs. are 7-string gtrs. tuned:
(Note: The bottom 6 strings use standard tuning, down a minor 3rd)

⑦=C♯ ③=G♯
⑥=F♯ ②=C♯
⑤=B   ①=C♯
④=E

Moderate rock ♩ = 116

Intro:

F♯5

1. *It's just   one of those*

Gtr. 1   **Rhy. Fig. 1**   **end Rhy. Fig. 1**

*Music sounds a minor 3rd lower than indicated.

Verse:

w/Rhy. Fig. 1 *(Gtr. 1) 4 times*

days   where you don't wan-na wake up.   Ev-'ry-thing is___ f***ed, ev-'ry-bod-y___ sucks.
2. *See additional lyrics*

You don't real-ly know why,   but you wan-na jus - ti-fy___   rip-pin' some-one's head off.

No hu-man con-tact,   and if you in - ter-act,___   your life is on con-tract.

Your best bet is to___ stay a-way, moth-er___ f***-er.   It's just one of those days.

†Please Note: Even though this song is arranged (as performed) for 7-string guitar, the song works easily on standard 6-string guitar.
The bottom 6 strings are actually standard tuning, down a step and a half. The added string (the highest) just doubles the regular high
E string. So the bottom six lines of tab work perfectly for standard 6-string guitar.

Break Stuff - 5 - 1

24

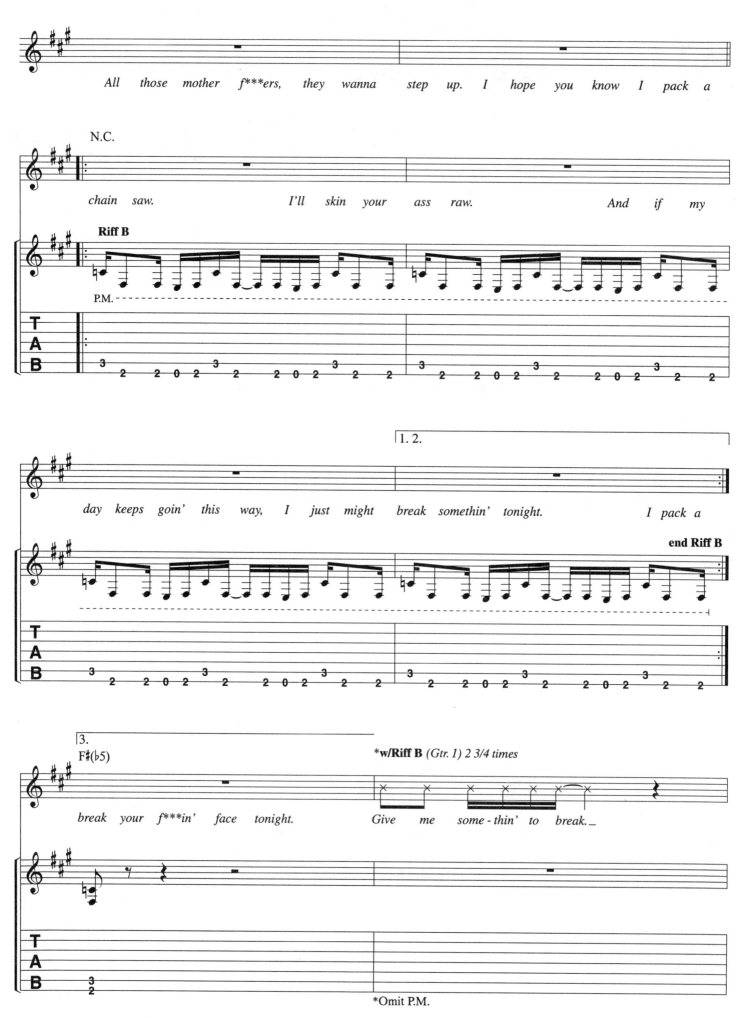

All those mother f***ers, they wanna step up. I hope you know I pack a

chain saw. I'll skin your ass raw. And if my

Riff B

P.M.

day keeps goin' this way, I just might break somethin' tonight. I pack a

end Riff B

F#(♭5)

break your f***in' face tonight. Give me some-thin' to break.

*w/**Riff B** *(Gtr. 1) 2 3/4 times*

*Omit P.M.

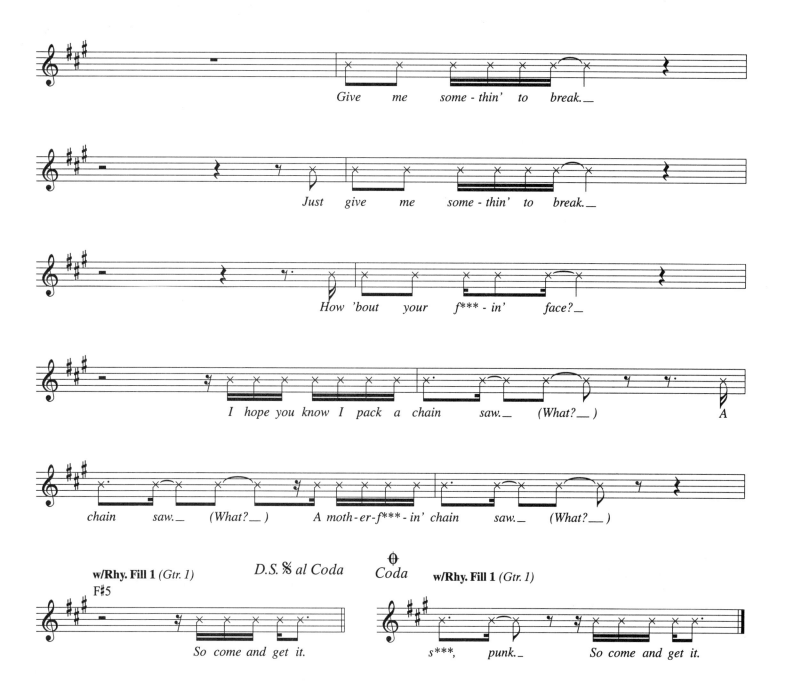

Verse 2:
It's just one of those days, feelin' like a freight train.
First one to complain leaves with a blood stain.
Damn right, I'm a maniac.
You better watch your back 'cause I'm f***in' up your program.
And if you're stuck-up,
You just lucked up, next in line to get f***ed up.
Your best bet is to stay away, mother f***er.
It's just one of those days.
(To Chorus:)

BACK TO SCHOOL
(Mini Maggit)

Words and Music by
CAMILO "CHINO" MORENO,
CHI CHENG, ABE CUNNINGHAM
and STEPHEN CARPENTER

Bb5   D5   G5   F#5

Tune down one whole step w/dropped D tuning:

⑥= C   ③= F
⑤= G   ②= A
④= C   ①= D

Moderately ♩ = 90

Intro:

Elec. Gtr. 1 N.C.
(clean-tone)

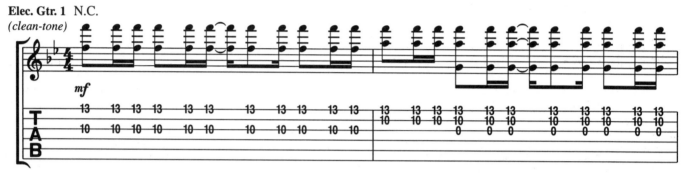

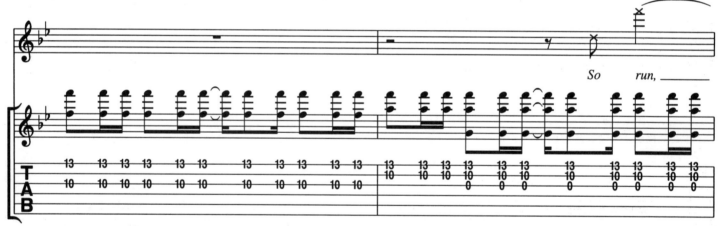

So run,

Elec. Gtr. 2
(w/dist.)   Bb5   D5   Bb5   D5

Cont. rhy. simile

right,

Elec. Gtr. 1
Rhy. Fig. 1

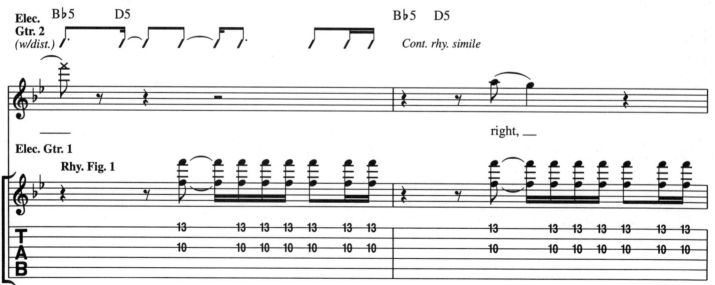

Back to School – 6 – 1

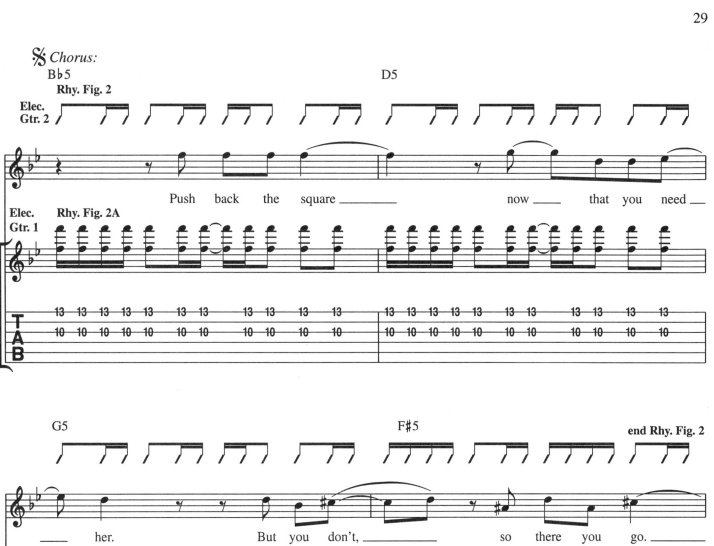

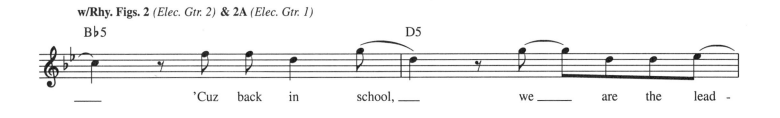

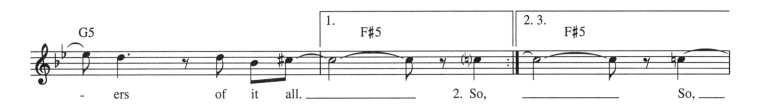

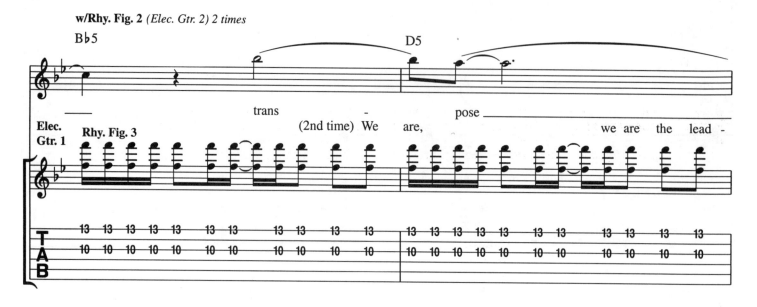

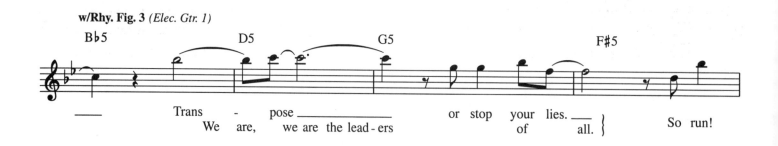

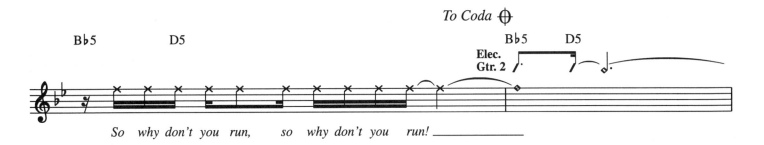

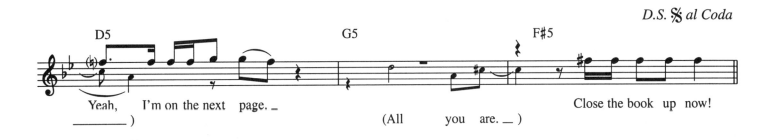

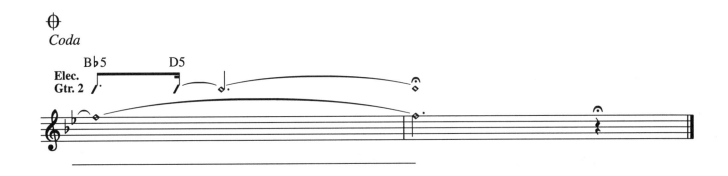

Back to School – 6 – 6

BAD RELIGION

Words and Music by
SULLY ERNA and TOMMY STEWART

Bad Religion - 4 - 1

From a bro - ken na - ti - on._____ It's a
re - li - gion, bad____ re - li - gion.____ A bro - ken na - tion.____

con - tra - dic - tion. _____
)
Yeah. ____

Gtr. 1

steady gliss.

Interlude
band tacet
Gtr. 1 tacet
Gtr. 2 (dist.)
*Gtrs. 1 & 2

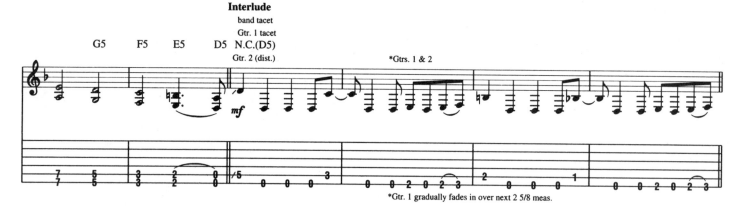

*Gtr. 1 gradually fades in over next 2 5/8 meas.

band enters

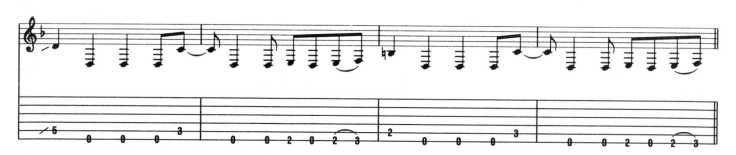

CHANGE
(IN THE HOUSE OF FLIES)

Words and Music by
CAMILO "CHINO" MORENO,
CHI CHENG, ABE CUNNINGHAM
and STEPHEN CARPENTER

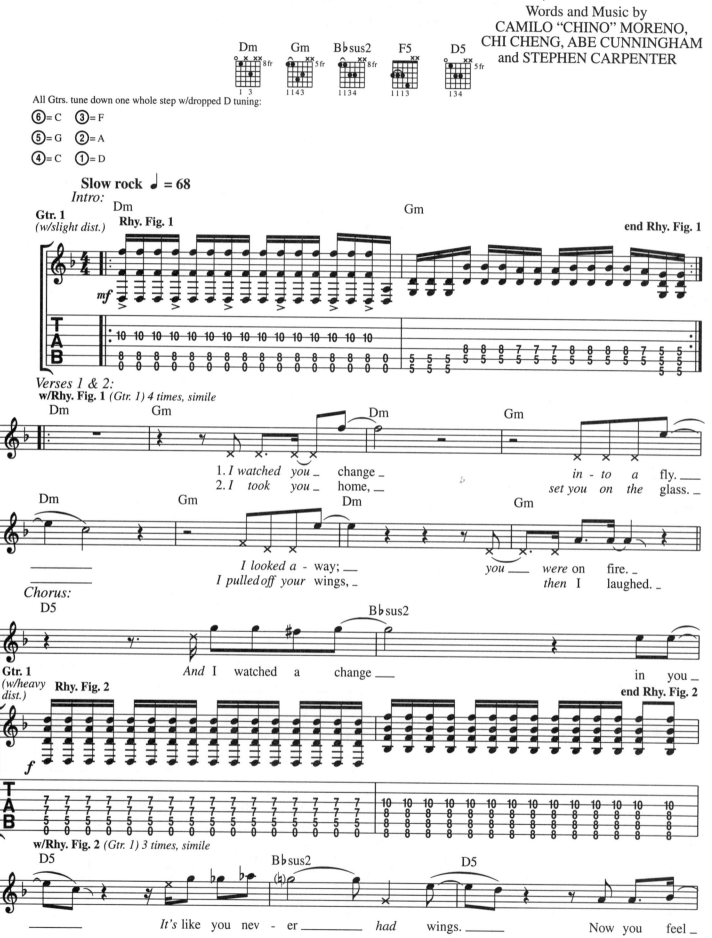

38

Change (In the House of Flies) – 4 – 3

Change (In the House of Flies) – 4 – 4

COWBOY

Words and Music by
ROBERT "KID ROCK" RITCHIE,
JOHN TRAVIS, MATTHEW SHAFER
and JAMES KENNETH TROMBLY

42

nest in the hills, chill _ like Flynt. _ Buy an old drop - top and find a spot to pimp. _ Then I'm a-

Kid Rock it up and down your block _ with a bot-tle of scotch _ and watch lots of crotch. _ Buy a

yacht with a flag say-ing, "chill-ing the most." _ Then rock that bitch up and down the coast. _ Give a

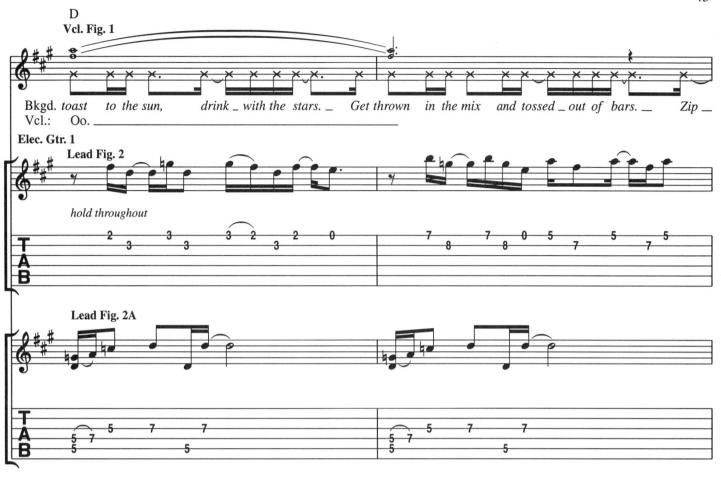

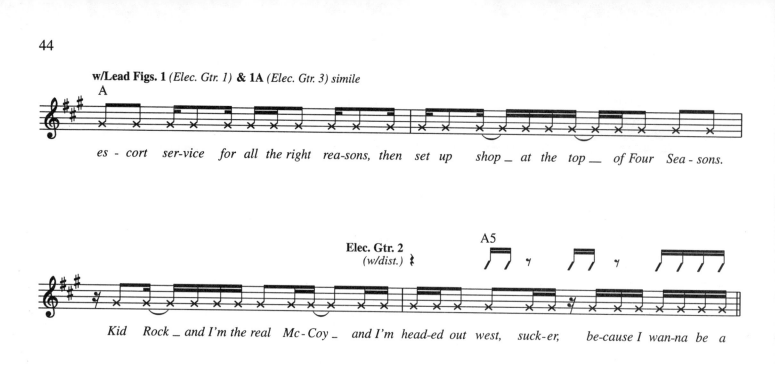

w/Lead Figs. 1 *(Elec. Gtr. 1)* & 1A *(Elec. Gtr. 3)* simile

es - cort ser-vice for all the right rea-sons, then set up shop _ at the top _ of Four Sea - sons.

Elec. Gtr. 2
(w/dist.)

Kid Rock _ and I'm the real Mc - Coy _ and I'm head-ed out west, suck-er, be-cause I wan-na be a

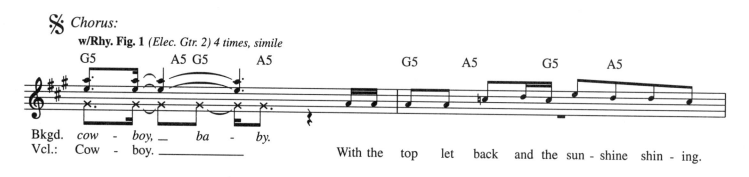

Chorus:

w/Rhy. Fig. 1 *(Elec. Gtr. 2)* 4 times, simile

Bkgd. *cow - boy, _ ba - by.*
Vcl.: Cow - boy. _____ With the top let back and the sun - shine shin - ing.

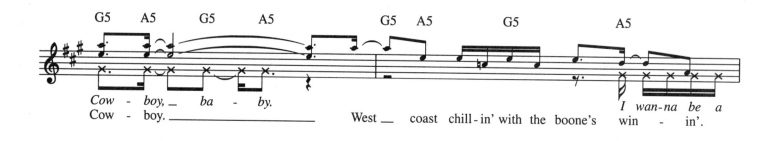

Cow - boy, _ ba - by.
Cow - boy. _____ West _ coast chill - in' with the boone's win - in'. I wan-na be a

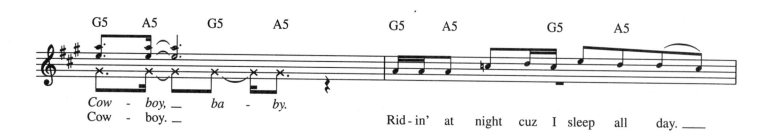

Cow - boy, _ ba - by.
Cow - boy. _ Rid - in' at night cuz I sleep all day. __

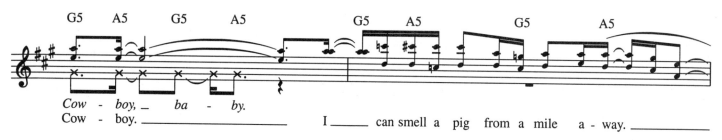

Cow - boy, _ ba - by.
Cow - boy. _____ I _____ can smell a pig from a mile a - way. _____

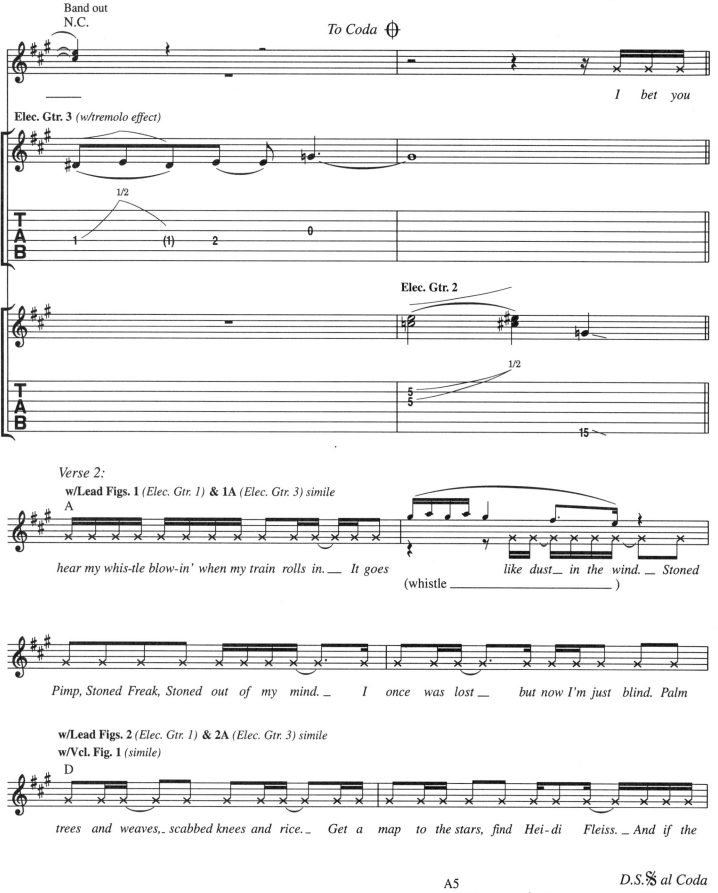

Band out
N.C.

To Coda ⊕

I bet you

Elec. Gtr. 3 *(w/tremolo effect)*

Elec. Gtr. 2

Verse 2:
w/Lead Figs. 1 *(Elec. Gtr. 1)* & **1A** *(Elec. Gtr. 3) simile*

hear my whis-tle blow-in' when my train rolls in. __ It goes   like dust __ in the wind. __ Stoned
(whistle _____)

Pimp, Stoned Freak, Stoned out of my mind. __   I once was lost __   but now I'm just blind. Palm

w/Lead Figs. 2 *(Elec. Gtr. 1)* & **2A** *(Elec. Gtr. 3) simile*
w/Vcl. Fig. 1 *(simile)*

trees and weaves, _ scabbed knees and rice. _   Get a map to the stars, find Hei- di   Fleiss. _ And if the

A5   *D.S.% al Coda*

Elec. Gtr. 2 *(w/dist.)*

price is right, _ then I'm-a make my   bid, _ boy, and let Cal- i-porn-i - yay _ know why they call   me

46

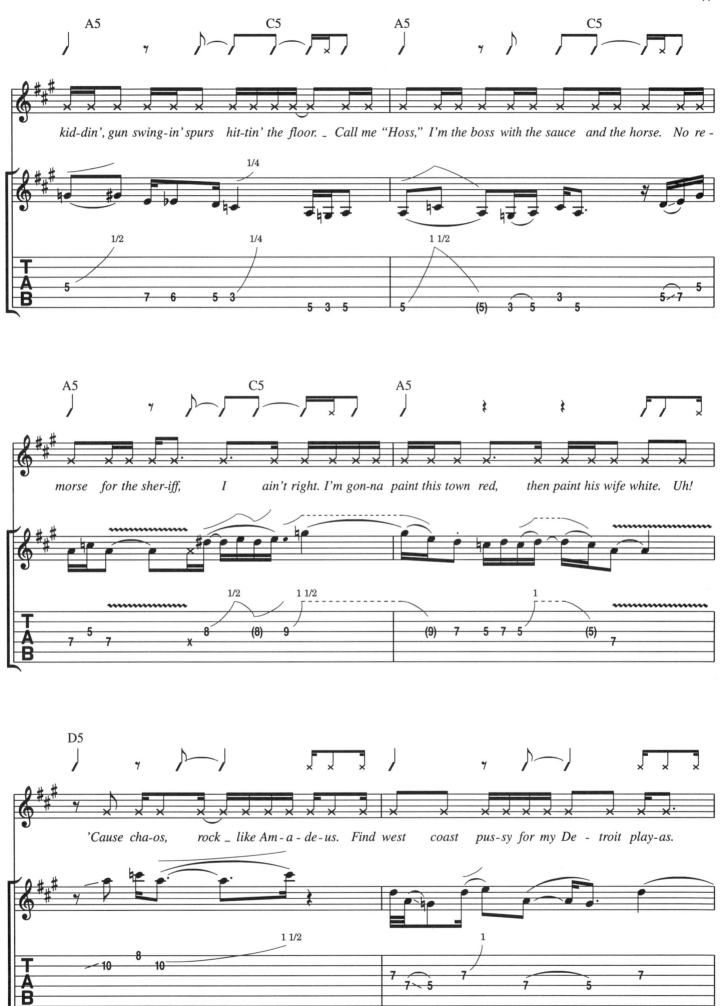

48

Mack like may-ors, ball _ like Lak-ers. They told us to leave but bet _ they can't make us.

grad. bend/hold

A.H.

Elec. Gtr. 2

Cont. in slashes

Why they wan-na pick on me, _ lock me up _ and snort a-way my key? I

partial A.H.

ain't no G, _ I'm just a reg-u-lar fail-ure. I ain't straight out of Comp-ton. I'm straight out the trail-er. Cuss _

Cowboy – 12 – 10

Chorus:

w/Rhy. Fig. 1 *(Gtr. 2) 6 times, simile*
Vcl. Fig. 2

end Vcl. Fig. 2

Bkgd.
Vcl.: Cow - boy. ___

With his top let back and the sun - shine shin - ing.

w/Vcl. Fig. 2 *(6 times) simile*

Spend all ___ my time ___ in Hol - ly-wood and Vine. ___

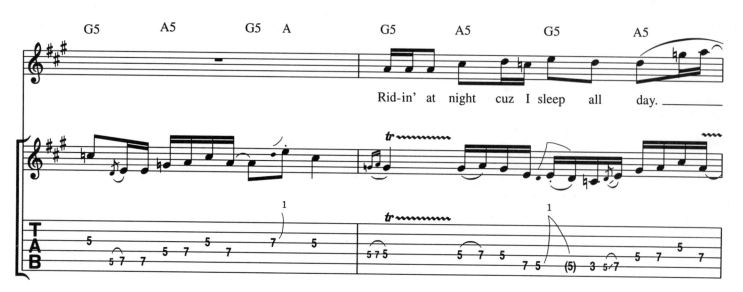

Rid-in' at night cuz I sleep all day. ___

DOWN

Words and Music by
DEAN DELEO, ROBERT DELEO,
ERIC KRETZ and SCOTT WEILAND

Drop D tuning:

⑥ = D ③ = G
⑤ = A ② = B
④ = D ① = E

Moderately fast rock ♩ = 136
Half-time feel
Intro:

54

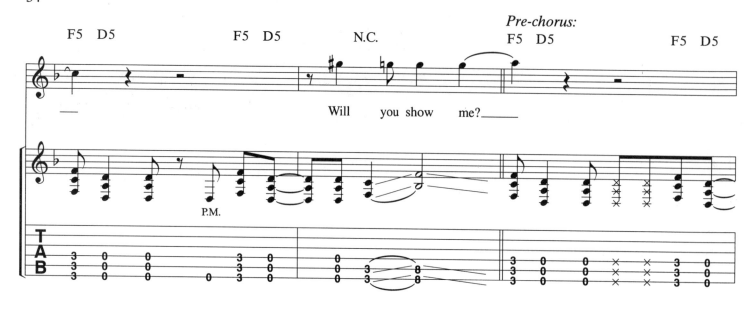

Will you show me?_____

I've been wait - in'_____ a long time now._____

*Harm. located between 2nd & 3rd frets.

— No, is the an - swer._____

harm.-----------------

Down - 9 - 3

56

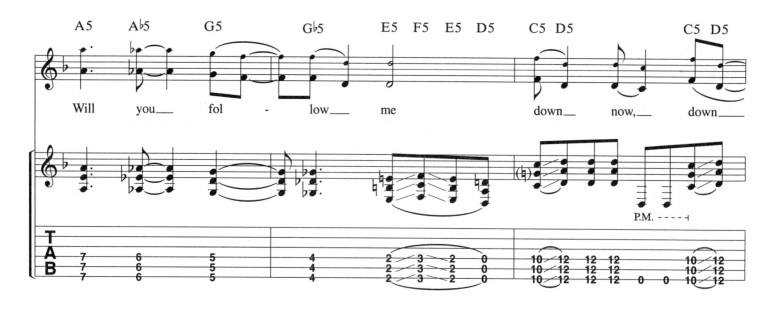

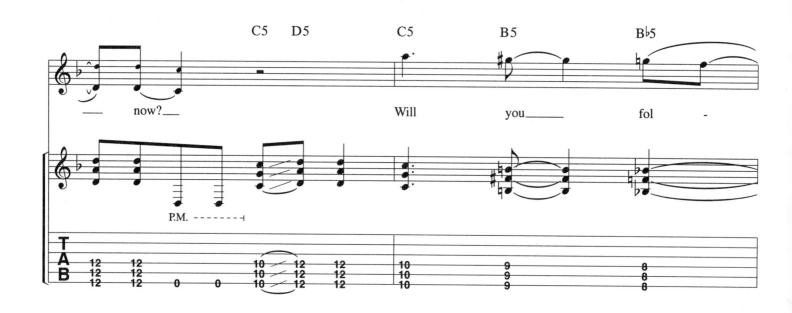

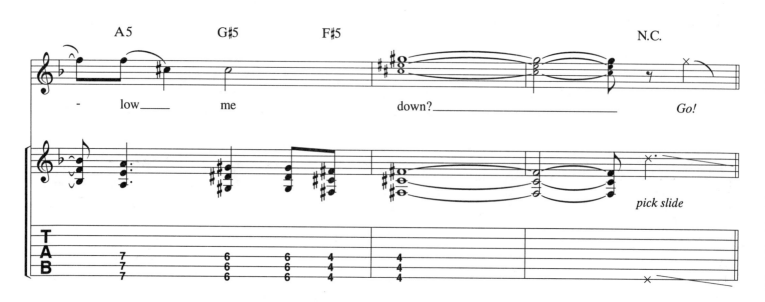

Down - 9 - 5

Guitar Solo:
w/Rhy. Fig. 1 *(Elec. Gtr. 1) 1st 4 meas., 3 times*

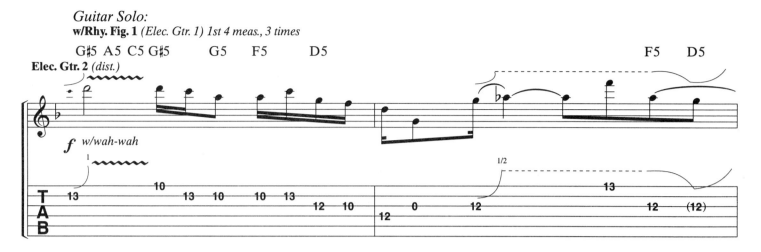

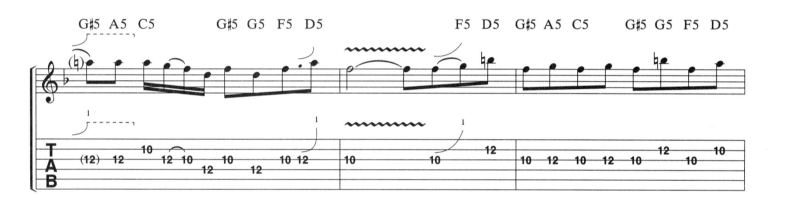

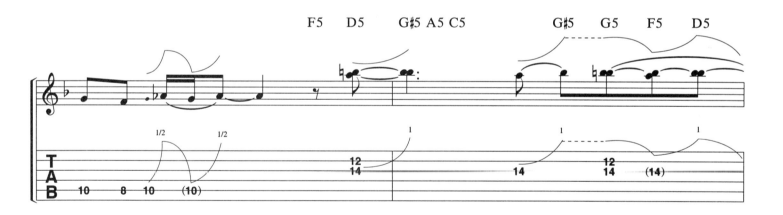

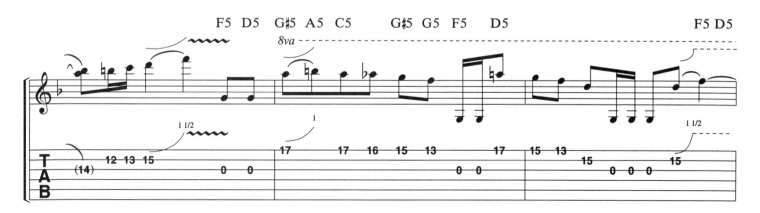

58

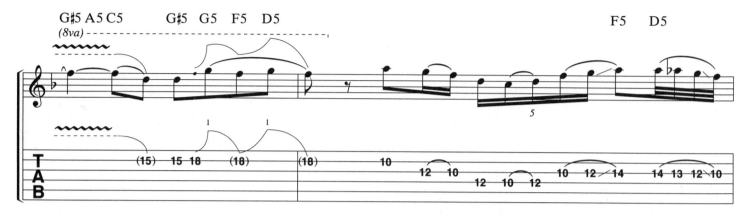

w/Rhy. Fig. 1 *(Elec. Gtr. 1) last 4 meas.*

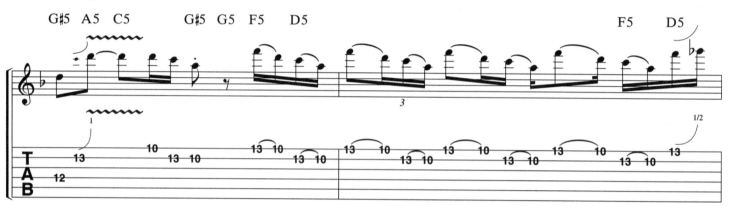

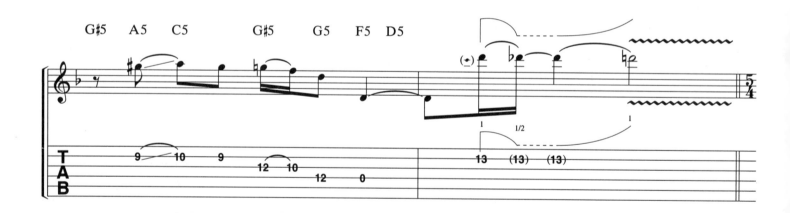

Interlude:
Elec. Gtr. 2 tacet

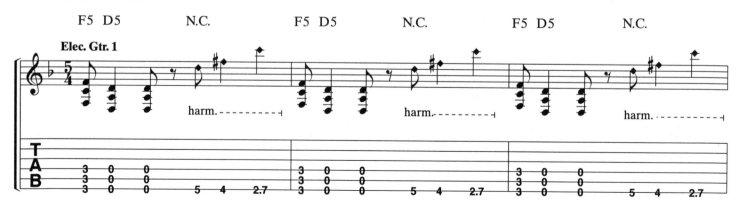

Down - 9 - 7

Chorus:
w/Rhy. Fig. 1 *(Elec. Gtr. 1) 1st 4 meas., 3 times*

Yeah,_____ I been__ wait-in' for my

Sun - day girl._____ Yeah,_____ I been__ wait-in' for my

Sun - day girl,_____ now._____ Yeah,_____

w/Rhy. Fig. 1 *(Elec. Gtr. 1)*
last 4 meas.

__ I been__ wait-in' for my Sun - day girl.__ Yeah,_____

__ I been__ wait-in' for my Sun - day girl,_____ now._____

Down - 9 - 8

60

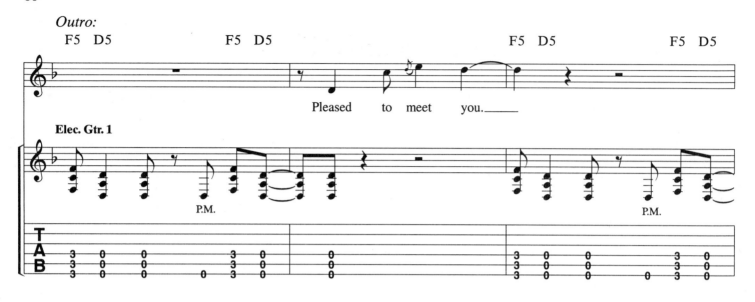

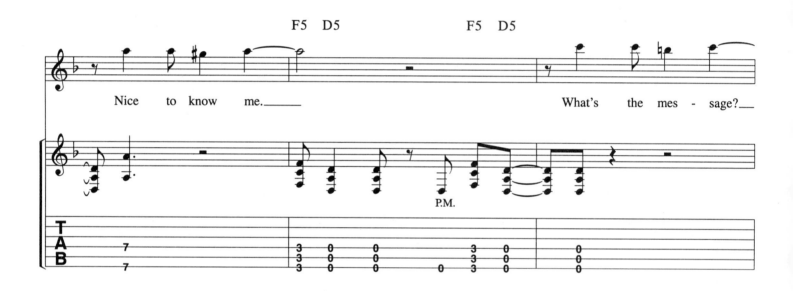

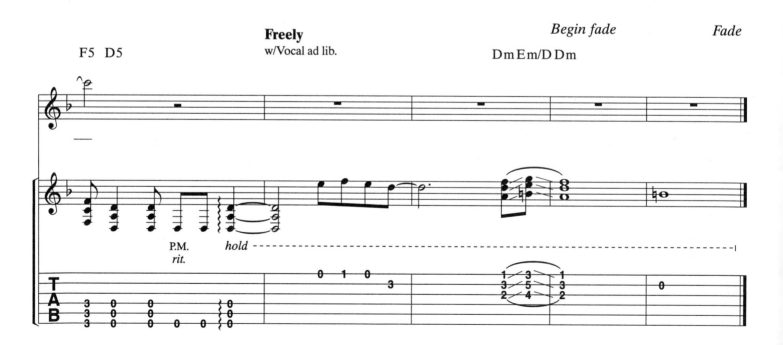

Down - 9 - 9

EX-GIRLFRIEND

Words and Music by
GWEN STEFANI, TOM DUMONT
and TONY KANAL

Ex-Girlfriend - 15 - 1

*Chord symbols indicate overall harmony; see frames under the title for suggested fingerings.

Verse 1:

64

Ex-Girlfriend - 15 - 4

66

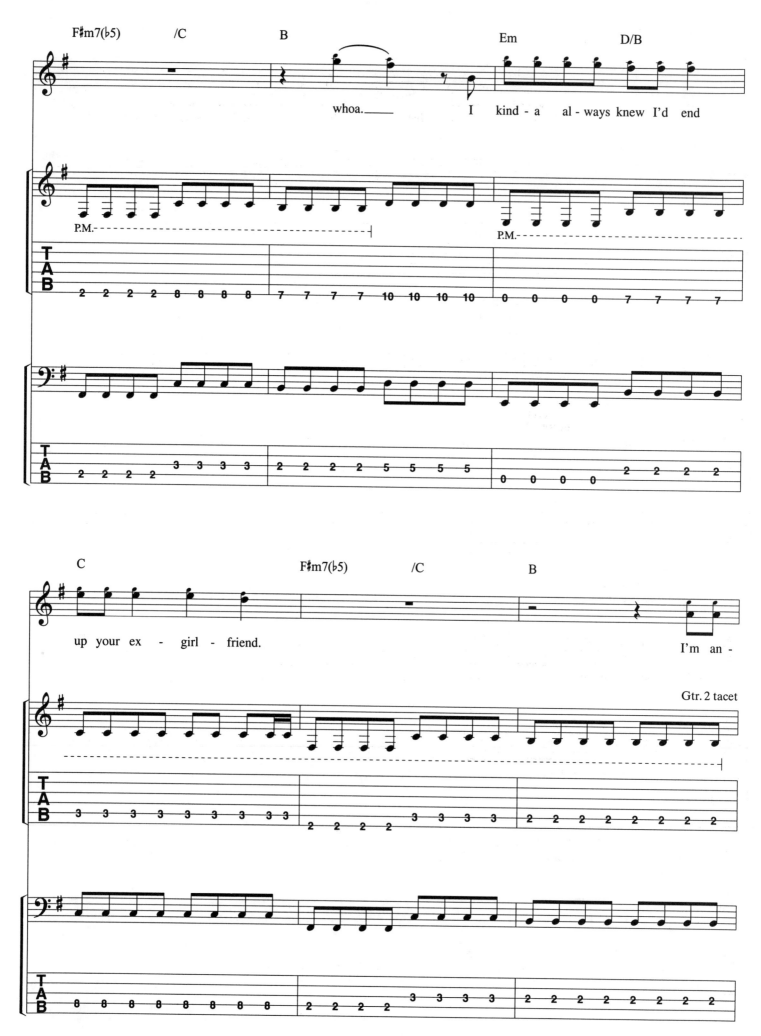

Ex-Girlfriend - 15 - 6

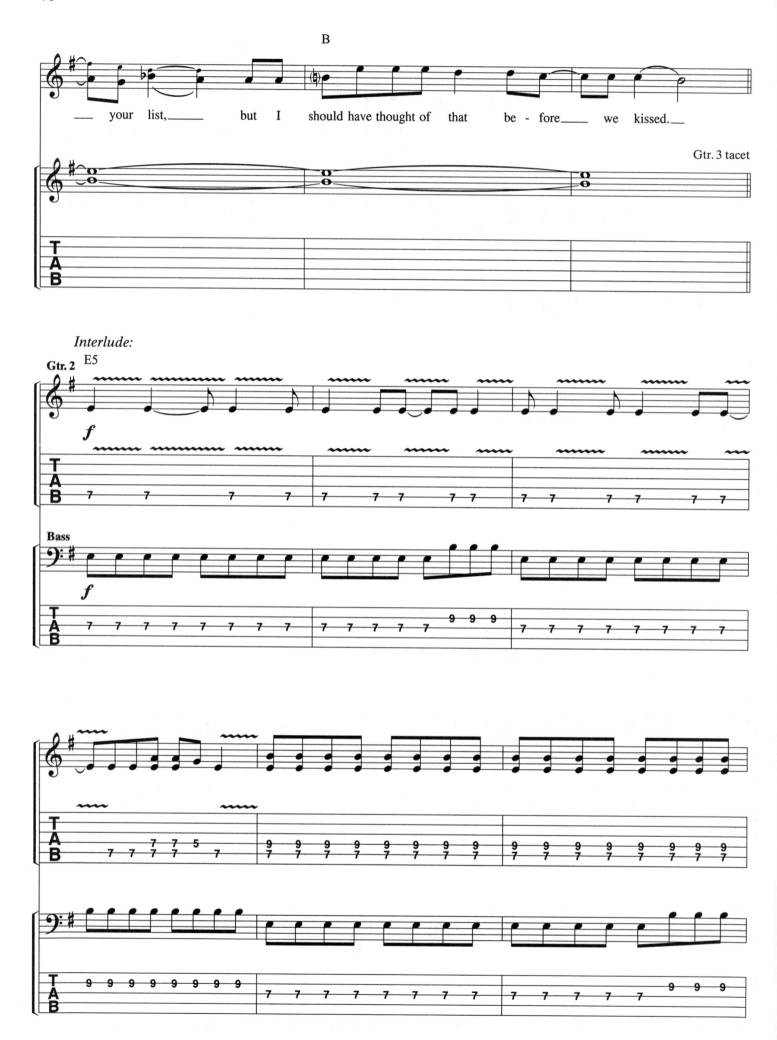

72

Ex-Girlfriend - 15 - 13

74

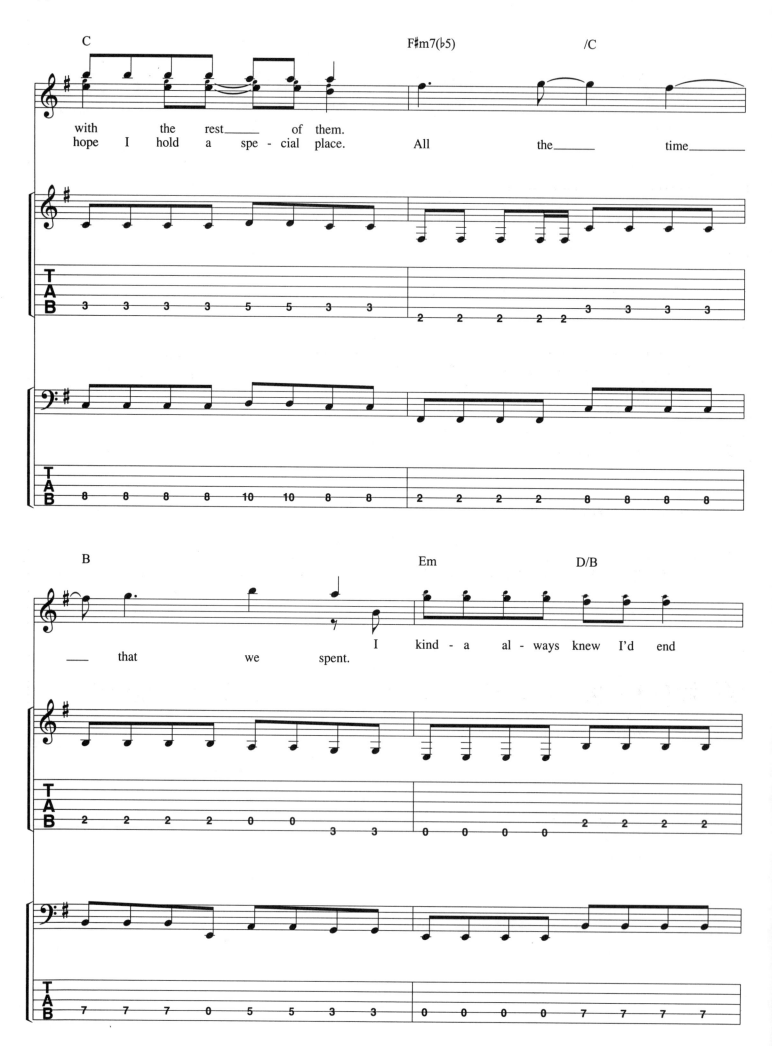

ENEMY

Open F#m tuning:
⑥=B ③=F#
⑤=F# ②=A
④=C# ①=C#

Words and Music by
TRAVIS MEEKS

Moderately ♩ = 116
w/Riff A (Gtr. 1) till it fades
w/Riff B (Gtr. 2) till it fades

Synth. Bass (arr. for gtr.)

(Bkgd. vcl.) Yeah.

Yeah!

Yeah.

Cont. synth. bass pattern

Yeah!

Yeah.

*Gtr. 1

Rhy. Fig. 1

*P.M. on ⑥.

Enemy - 10 - 1

78

Enemy - 10 - 3

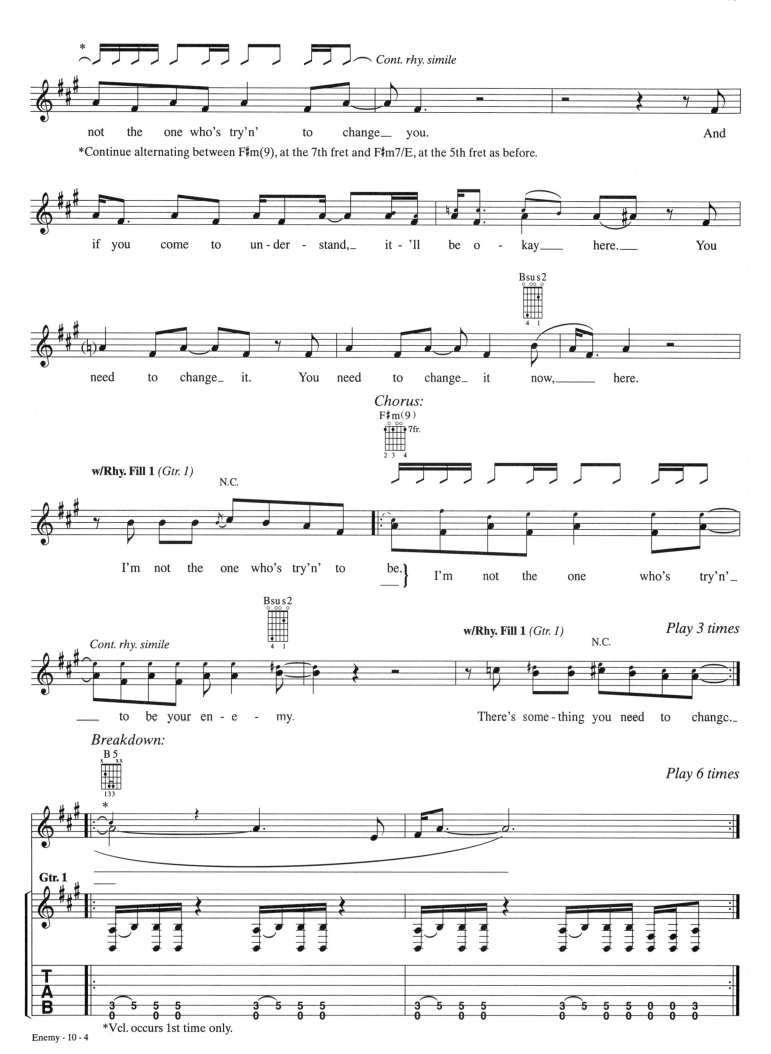

80

82

Cont. rhy. simile

your en - e - my.____

Rhy. Fig. 2

1.

I'm not the one who's try'n' to

2.

F♯m(9)
7fr.
2 3 4

your en - e - my.____

Gtrs. 1 & 2 cont. rhy. simile, till fade

1.

Your en - e - my.__

2.

Fade

Your en - e - my!__

Enemy - 10 - 7

*Fade continues through 1st bar of next section.

84

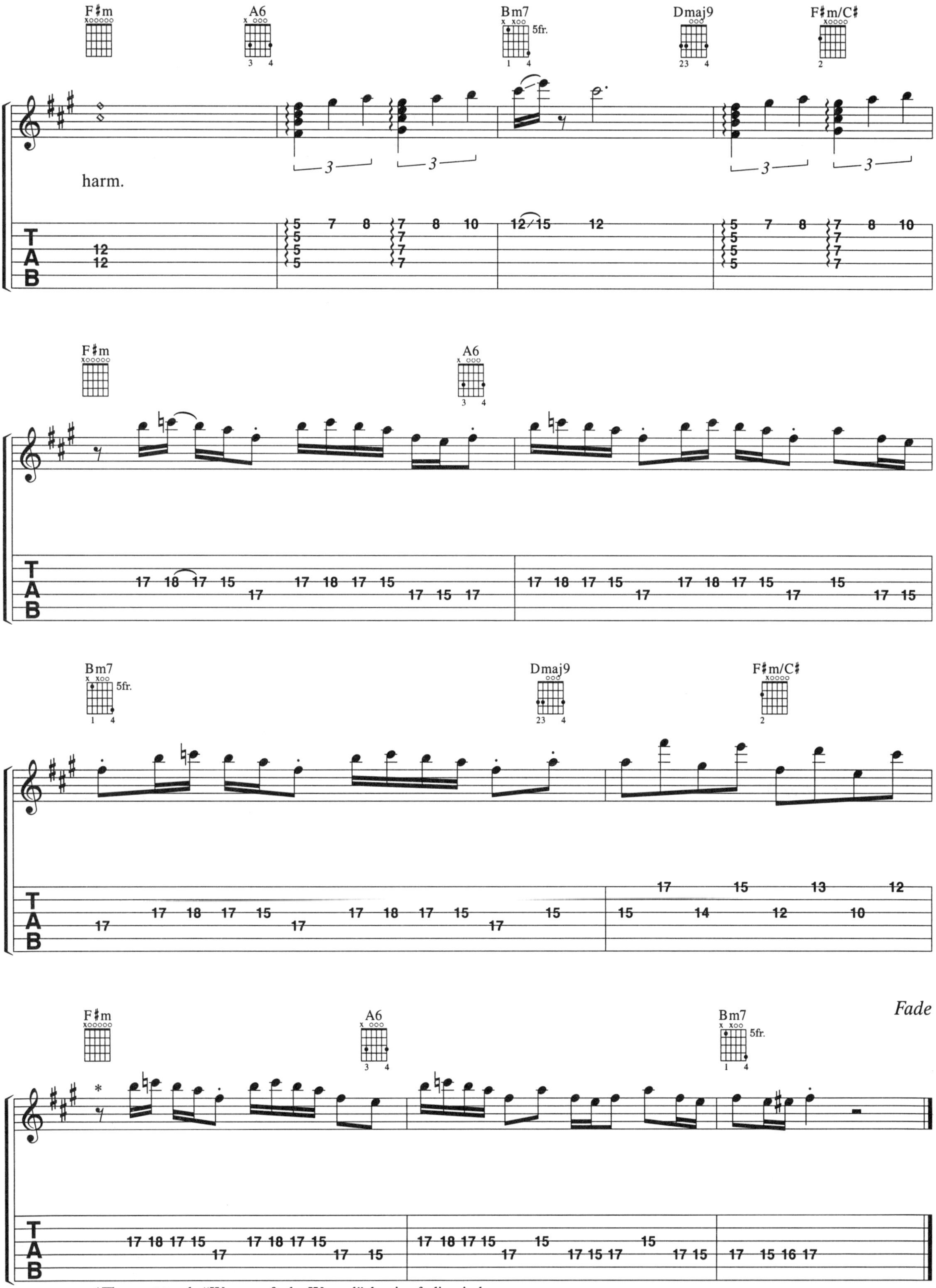

*The next track, "Weapon & the Wound", begins fading in here.

EVERYTHING YOU WANT

All gtrs. tuned down 1/2 step:

⑥ = E♭ ③ = G♭
⑤ = A♭ ② = B♭
④ = D♭ ① = E♭

Words and Music by
MATTHEW SCANNELL

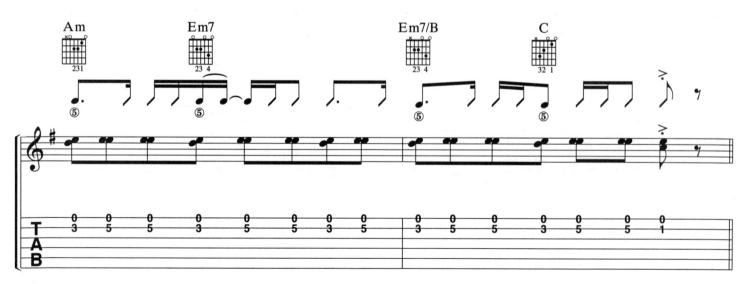

Verse 1:

w/Rhy. Fig. 1 *(Elec. Gtr. 1) 2 times, simile*

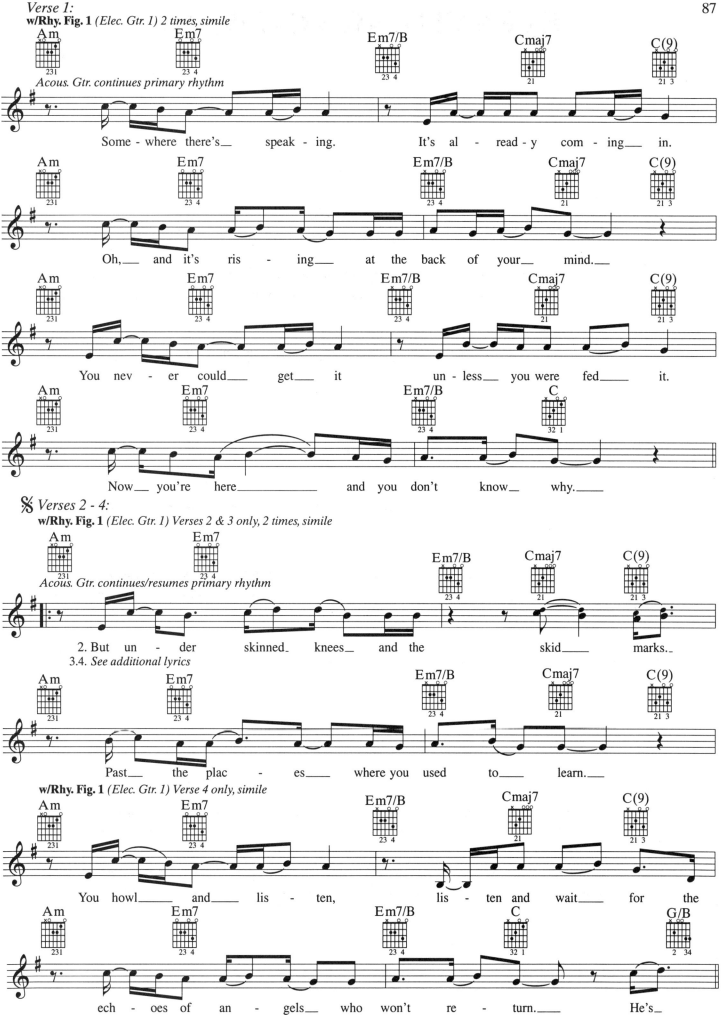

Acous. Gtr. continues primary rhythm

Some - where there's___ speak - ing. It's al - read - y com - ing___ in.

Oh,___ and it's ris - ing___ at the back of your___ mind.___

You nev - er could___ get___ it un - less___ you were fed___ it.

Now___ you're here_____ and you don't know___ why.___

Verses 2 - 4:

w/Rhy. Fig. 1 *(Elec. Gtr. 1) Verses 2 & 3 only, 2 times, simile*

Acous. Gtr. continues/resumes primary rhythm

2. But un - der skinned_ knees_ and the skid___ marks._

3.4. *See additional lyrics*

Past___ the plac - es___ where you used to___ learn.___

w/Rhy. Fig. 1 *(Elec. Gtr. 1) Verse 4 only, simile*

You howl___ and___ lis - ten, lis - ten and wait___ for the

ech - oes of an - gels___ who won't re - turn.___ He's___

Verse 3:
You're waiting for someone
To put you together.
You're waiting for someone
To push you away.
There's always another
Wound to discover.
There's always something more
You wish he'd say.
(To Chorus:)

Verse 4:
Out of the island,
Into the highway.
Past the places where you might have turned.
You never did notice,
But you still hide away
The anger of angels who won't return.
(To Chorus:)

FALLING AWAY FROM ME

Chord frames for slash notation

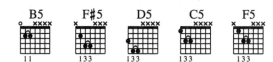

All gtrs. are 7-string gtrs.
tuned down 1 whole step:

⑦ = A ③ = F

⑥ = D ② = A

⑤ = G ① = D

④ = C

Moderately ♩ = 108

Intro:

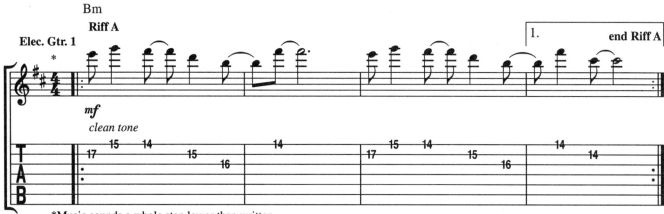

*Music sounds a whole step lower than written.

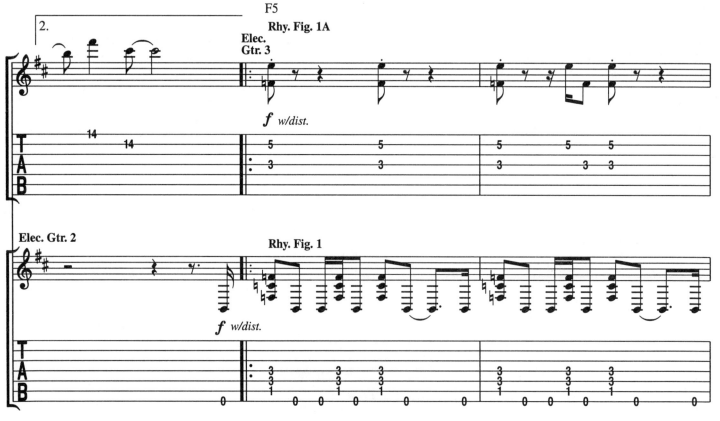

Falling Away From Me – 5 – 1

Verse:

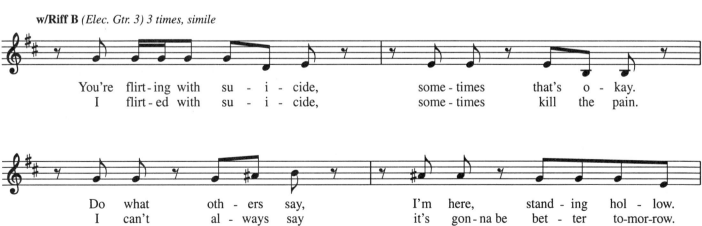

94

Falling Away From Me – 5 – 3

HEAVEN & HOT RODS

Words and Music by
DEAN DELEO, ROBERT DELEO,
ERIC KRETZ and SCOTT WEILAND

Drop D tuning:

⑥ = D ③ = G
⑤ = A ② = B
④ = D ① = E

Moderate rock ♩ = 128

Intro:

A5 G5 G#5 A5   C5 C#5 D5   A5 G#5 G5   E5 E♭5 D5

Elec. Gtrs. 1 & 2
Rhy. Fig. 1

Drum

G5 G#5 A5   E5 E♭5 D5   1. G5 G#5 A5   D5 A5 D5   2. G5 G#5 A5 N.C.

end Rhy. Fig. 1

𝄋 Verse:

A5 G5 G#5 A5   C5 C#5 D5   A5 G#5 G5   E5 E♭5 D5   G5 G#5 A5   E5 E♭5 D5

1.3. You can___ get it   if___ you real-ly want it, but you're bet-ter off, just leave it a-lone.___
2. You don't___ get it,   no,___ you won't for-get it. You're bet-ter off, just leave it a-lone.___

G5 G#5 A5 D5 A5 D5 A5   G5 G#5 A5   C5 C#5 D5   A5 G#5 G5   E5 E♭5 D5

___   You won't for-get   it   if___ you ev-er had it, so you're
___   If you don't stop   think-in'   soon,___ you will be drink-in', and you're

Heaven & Hot Rods - 5 - 1

98

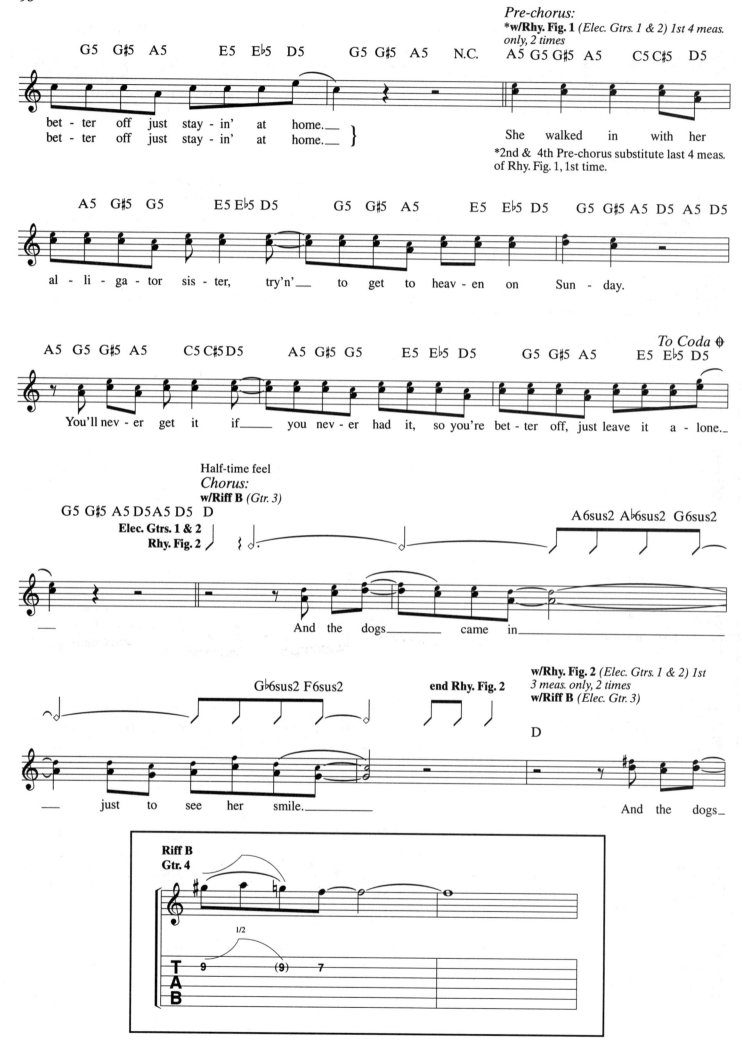

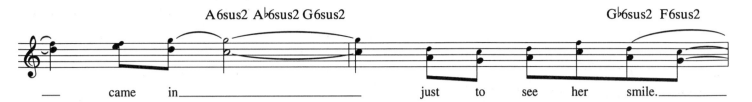

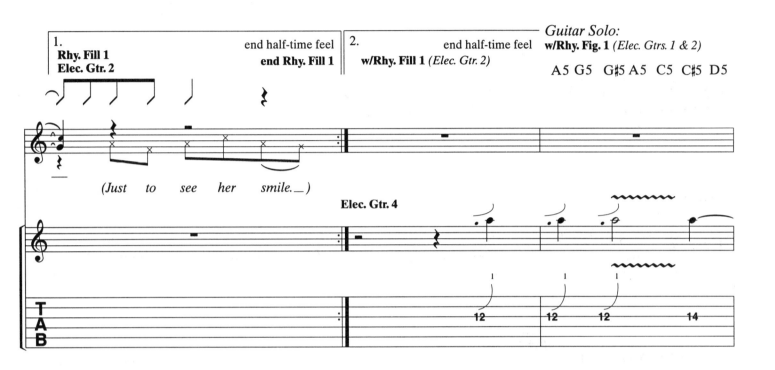

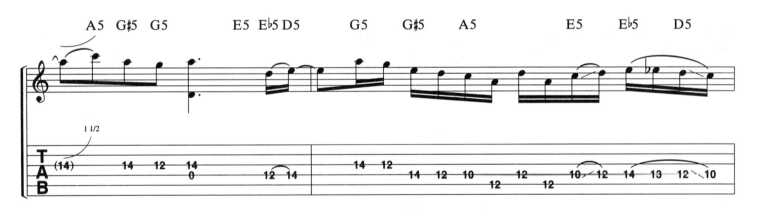

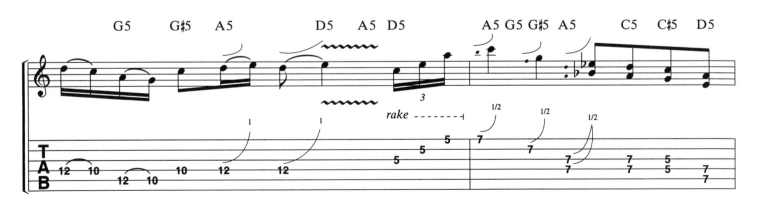

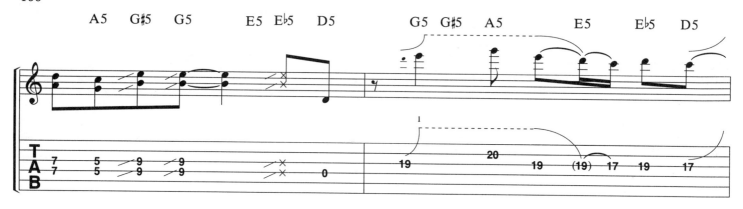

Pre-chorus:
w/Rhy. Fig. 1 *(Elec. Gtrs. 1 & 2) 1st 7 meas. only*
w/Riff A *(Elec. Gtr. 3)*

She walked in with her al - li - ga - tor sis - ter, try'n'_

Elec. Gtr. 4 out

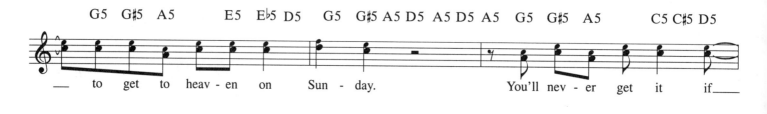

— to get to heav - en on Sun - day. You'll nev - er get it if___

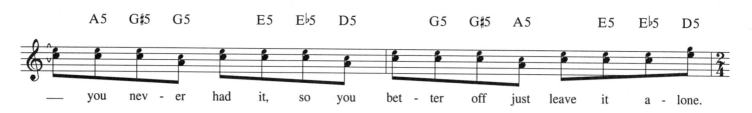

— you nev - er had it, so you bet - ter off just leave it a - lone.

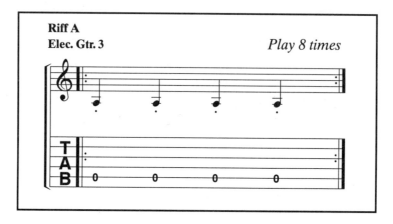

Riff A
Elec. Gtr. 3   *Play 8 times*

G5   G#5   A5

Half-time feel
Bridge:
Elec. Gtrs. 1 & 2
Rhy. Fig. 3
B5   Bb5   Dm   G5

Mom, I'm still___ heal - ing.___

(Com - ing___ down.___)

*Two gtrs. arr. for one; Elec. Gtr. 2 w/heavy tremolo (next 14 meas.).

w/Rhy. Fig. 3 *(Elec. Gtrs. 1 & 2)*
A   B5   Bb5   Dm   G5

end Rhy. Fig. 3

___   Oh, and I'm still___ breath - ing.___

(Com - ing___ down___)

w/Rhy. Fig. 3 *(Elec. Gtrs. 1 & 2)*
B5   Bb5   Dm

w/fdbk.   *D.S. %* al Coda

(Com - ing___ down.___)

w/Voc. ad lib.   *Play 4 times*
Coda G5 G#5 A5   G5 G#5 A5   G5 G#5 A5   G5 G#5 A5   G5 G#5 A5

Heaven & Hot Rods - 5 - 5

FALLS APART

Words and Music by MARK MCGRATH, STAN FRAZIER,
RODNEY SHEPPARD, MATTHEW MURPHY KARGES,
CRAIG BULLOCK, JOSEPH "MCG" BULLOCK and DAVID KAHNE

*Bass note played by Bass only (next three meas.).

Falls Apart – 6 – 1

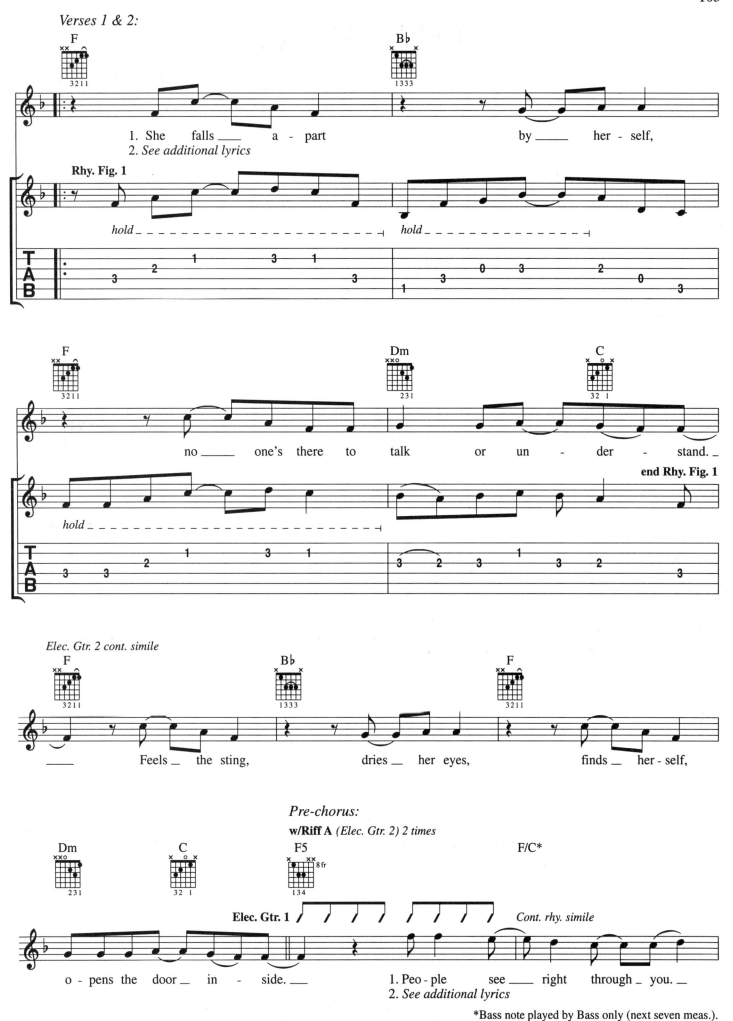

Falls Apart – 6 – 4

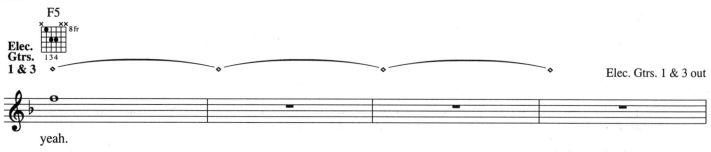

Verse 3:
w/Rhy. Fig. 1 *(Elec. Gtr. 2)*

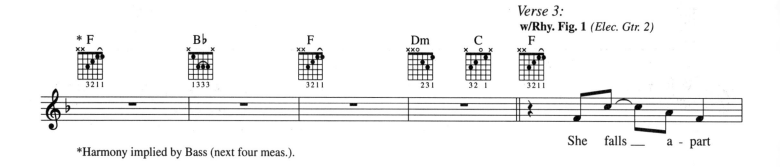

*Harmony implied by Bass (next four meas.).

Falls Apart – 6 – 5

*Bass note played by Bass only.

Verse 2:
You walk along by yourself.
There's no sound, nothing's changing.
They've gone away, left you there.
Emptiness, there's nothing you can share.
(To Pre-chorus 2:)

Pre-chorus 2:
All those words that hurt you, more than you would let it show.
It comes apart by itself, always will and everything's wasted.
(To Chorus:)

HEMORRHAGE

Lyrics and Music by
CARL BELL

Tune down 1/2 step:
⑥=E♭ ③=G♭
⑤=A♭ ②=B♭
④=D♭ ①=E♭

Slow rock ♩ = 76
Intro:

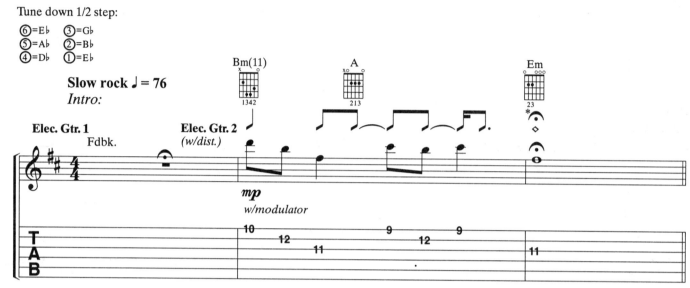

*Let note and chord ring over
next two measures.

Verse 1:

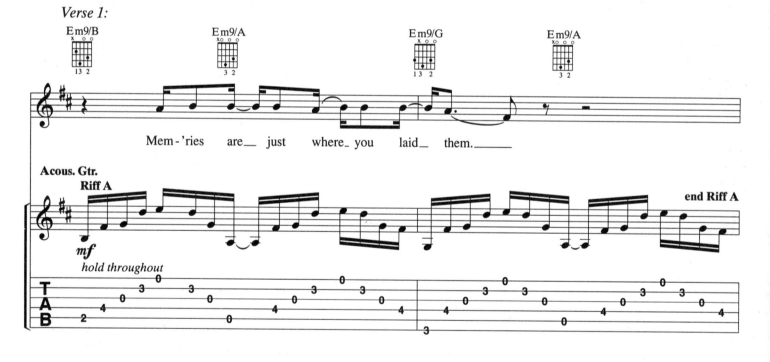

Mem-'ries are__ just where_ you laid__ them._____

Acous. Gtr.
Riff A

end Riff A

hold throughout

w/Riff A *(Acous. Gtr.) 3 times, simile*
Elec. Gtrs. 1 & 2 tacet

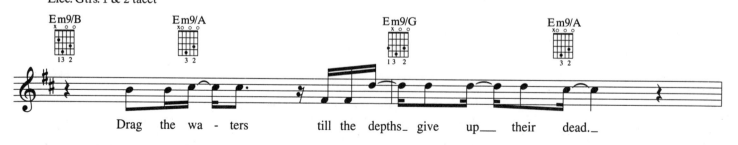

Drag the wa - ters till the depths_ give up__ their dead._

Hemorrhage - 9 - 1

110

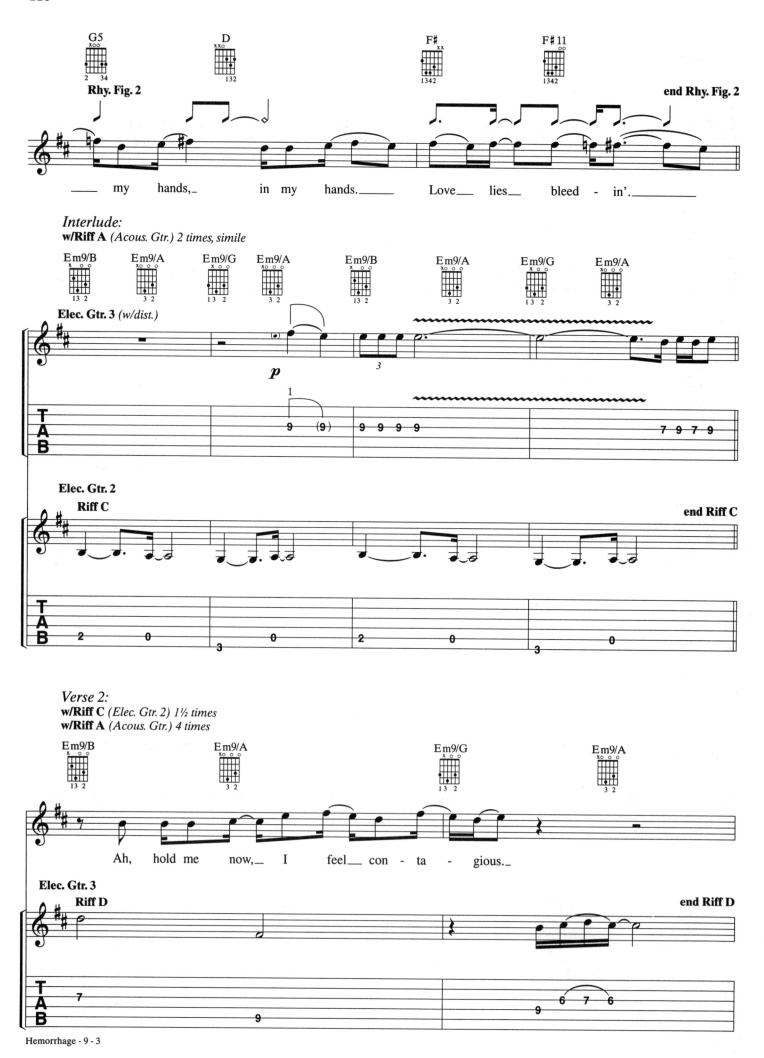

112

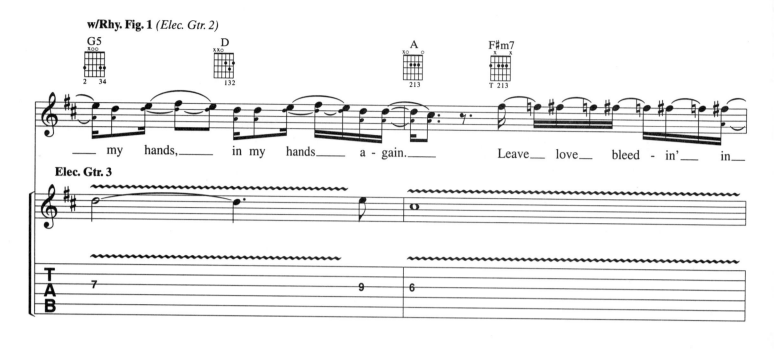

Hemorrhage - 9 - 5

114

Hemorrhage - 9 - 7

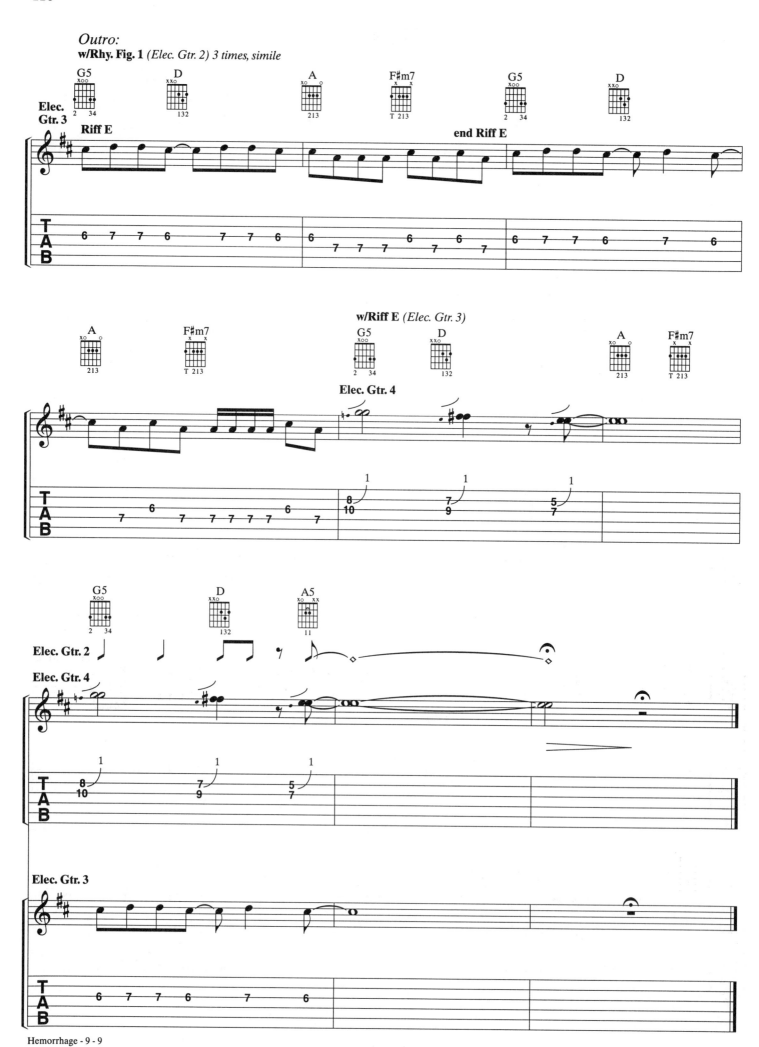

HOME

Words and Music by
MICHAEL MUSHOK, AARON LEWIS,
JOHN APRIL and JONATHAN WYSOCKI

Elec. Gtrs. 1 & 2
tuned down:
⑥ = A♭   ③ = D♭
⑤ = D♭   ② = G♭
④ = A♭   ① = B♭

Acous. Gtr. tuned down
1/2 step w/Drop D tuning:
⑥ = D♭   ③ = G♭
⑤ = A♭   ② = B♭
④ = D♭   ① = E♭

*Chord symbols reflect implied harmony.

1. I force my-self___ through an-oth-er   day.___   Can't ex-plain___ the way___ to - day___
2. An-oth-er sleep-less night a - gain.___   Ho-tel room's my on - ly   friend,___

Home - 5 - 1

118

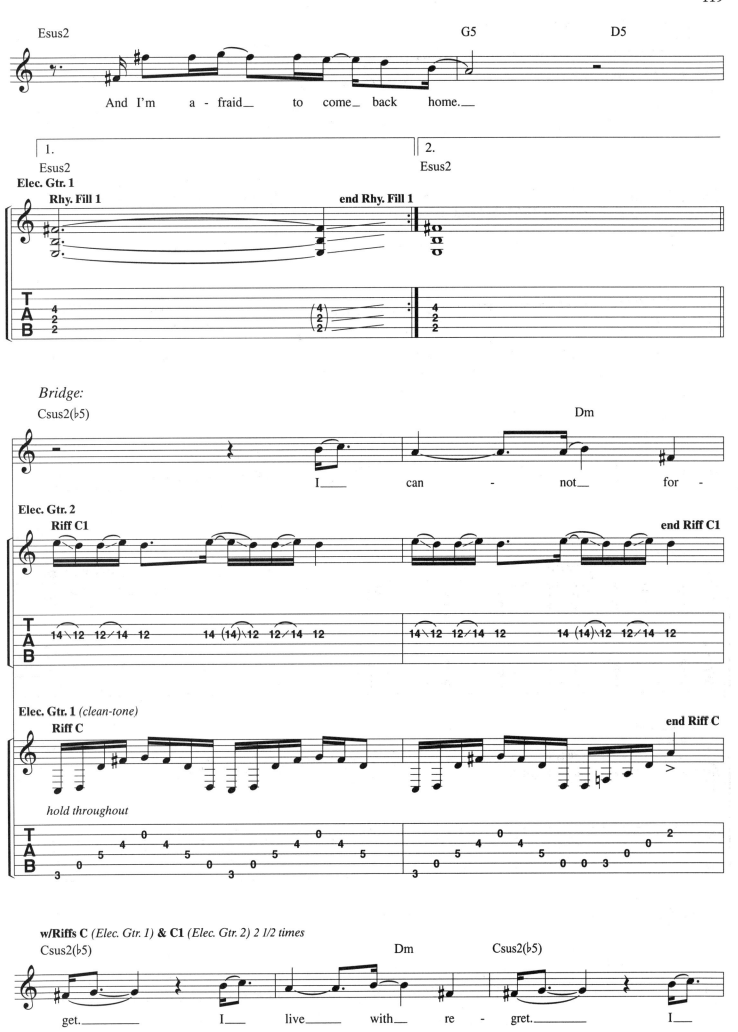

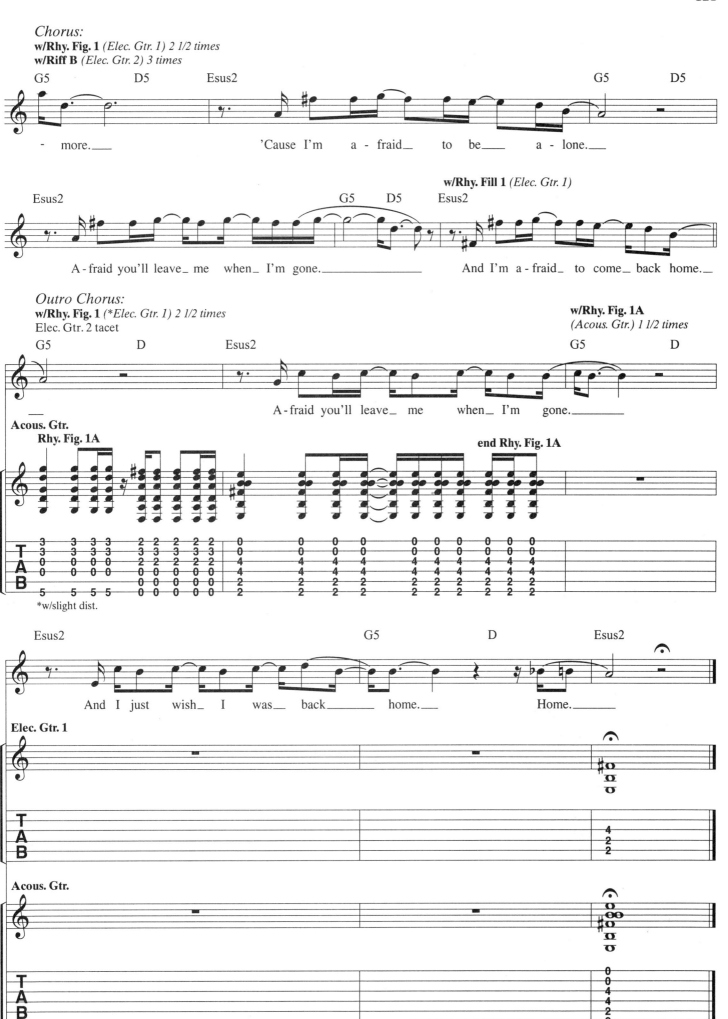

I WALK ALONE

Words and Music by
THOMAS FLOWERS, DOUG ELDRIDGE,
RIC IVANISEVICH and FRED NELSON, JR.

All Gtrs. tune down 1/2 step w/Dropped D tuning:

⑥ = D♭ ③ = G♭
⑤ = A♭ ② = B♭
④ = D♭ ① = E♭

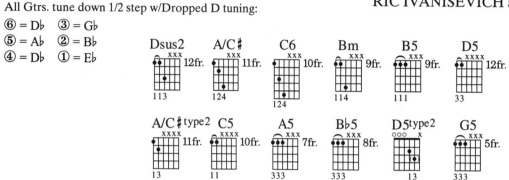

Moderately ♩ = 106

Verse 1:

I can't take_ it an-y more_ and I'm al-most pret-ty_

_ sure   I've_ been here be-fore._

w/Rhy. Fig. 1 (Elec. Gtr. 1) 2 3/4 times, simile

I can't take_ this an-y long-er, I won't heal_ un-til I'm strong-er,_

I Walk Alone - 7 - 1

I Walk Alone - 7 - 2

Interlude:

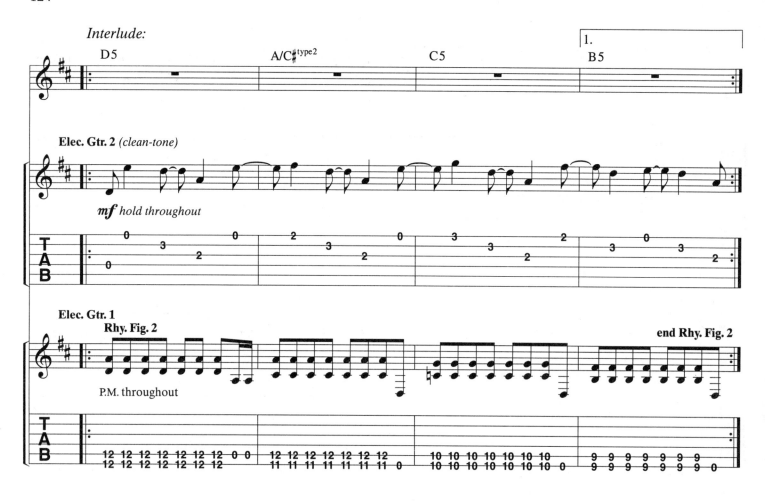

I Walk Alone - 7 - 4

126

I Walk Alone - 7 - 5

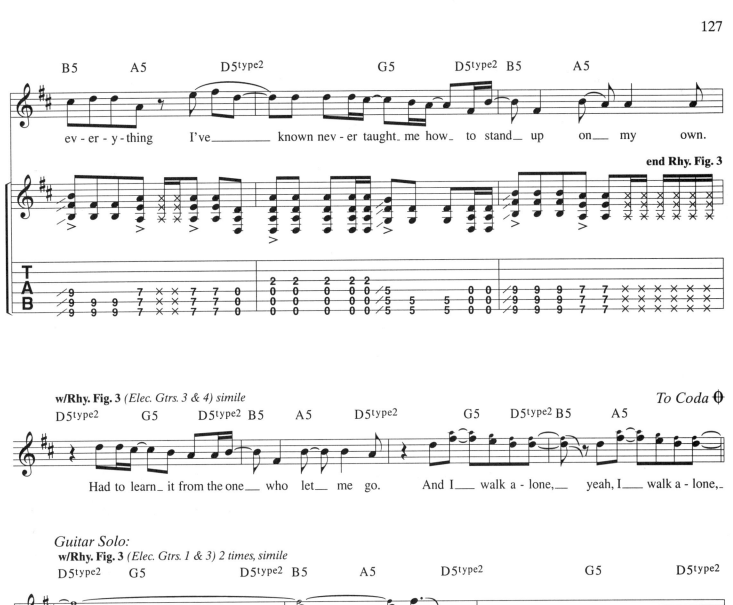

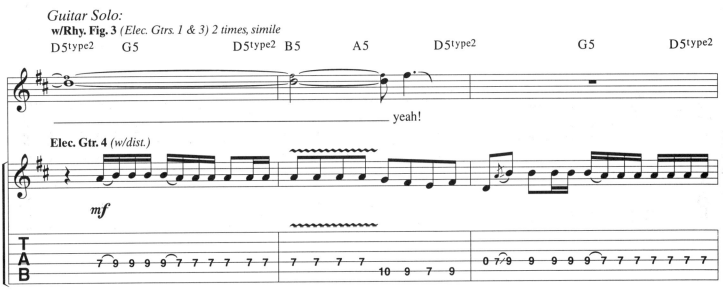

I Walk Alone - 7 - 6

128

I Walk Alone - 7 - 7

IN 2 DEEP

Words and Music by
KENNY WAYNE SHEPHERD,
MARK SELBY and DANNY TATE

*Composite arrangement.

In 2 Deep – 9 – 1

130

In 2 Deep – 9 – 2

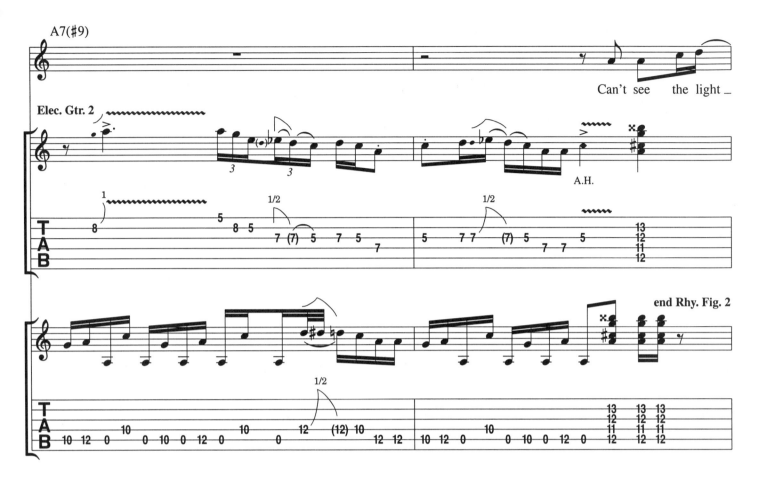

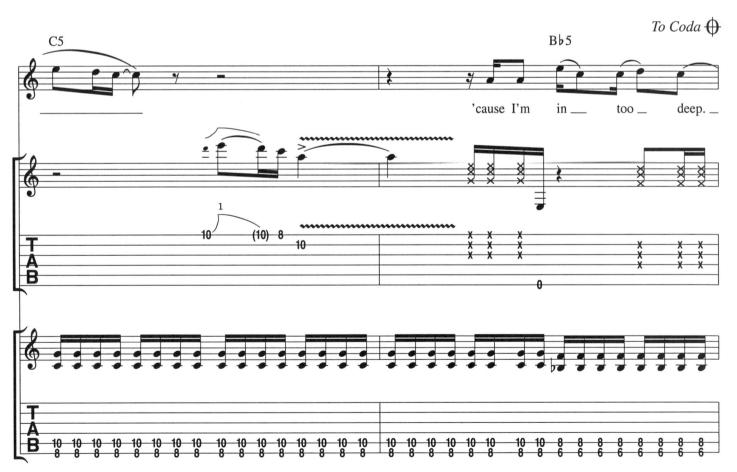

132

O - ver my head.

Rhy. Fig. 3

1.

end Rhy. Fig. 3

In 2 Deep – 9 – 4

134

O - ver _ my head. _

Whoa!

Elec. Gtr. 2

pp < mp

fdbk.

Guitar Solo:
Elec. Gtr. 2

B7(#9)

Elec. Gtr. 1

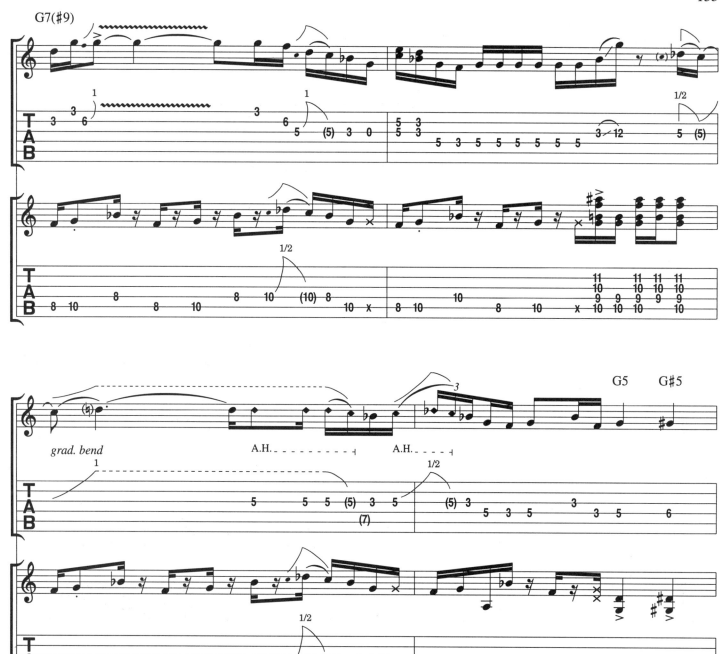

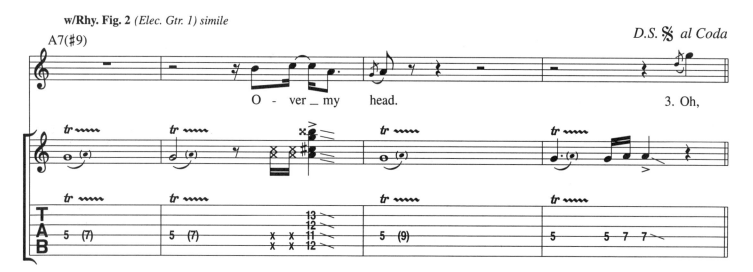

Coda

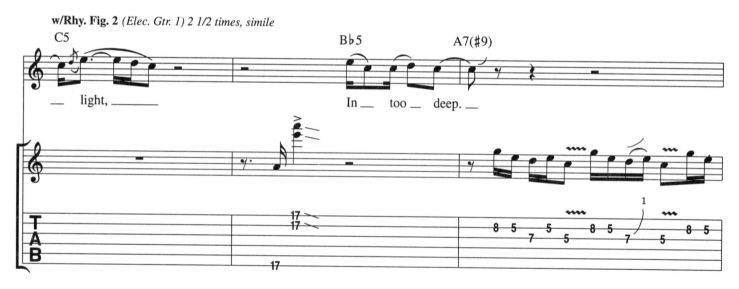

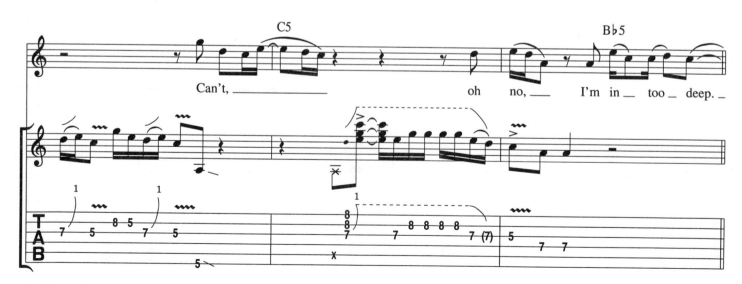

Outro:

w/Rhy. Fig. 3 *(Elec. Gtr. 1) 1 1/2 times, simile*

I'm o - ver _ my head. _   O - ver _ my head. _

O - ver _ my   head. _

Elec. Gtr. 2

Elec. Gtr. 1

Verse 3:
Oh, someone call somebody,
The asylum's under siege.
Inmates took a hostage,
I'll be damned if it's not me.
Nowhere to hide
'Cause I'm in too deep.
Bury the light
'Cause I'm in too deep.
Can't see the light,
In too deep.
Bury the light.
Oh, no I'm in too deep, oh.

KEEP AWAY

Words and Music by
SULLY ERNA

Keep Away - 6 - 1

140

Keep Away - 6 - 3

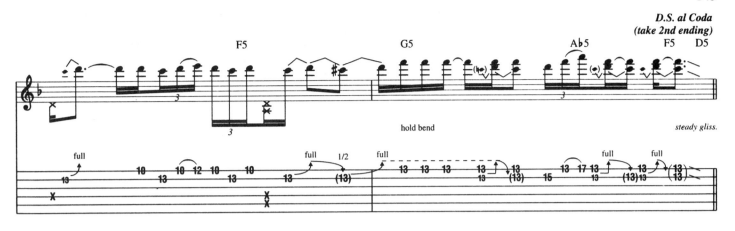

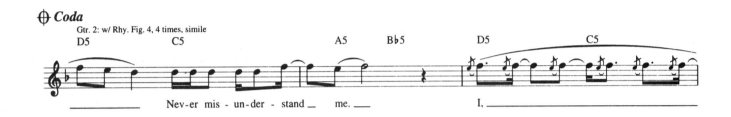

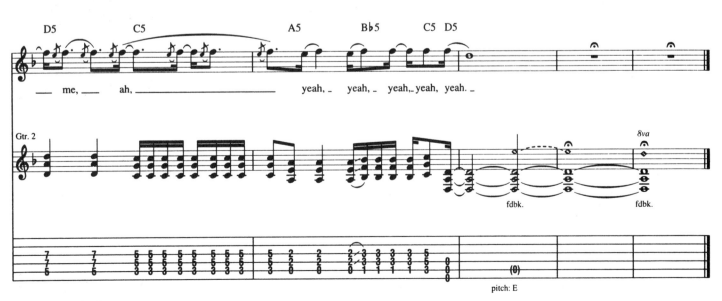

Keep Away - 6 - 6

KRYPTONITE

Music by MATT ROBERTS,
BRAD ARNOLD and TODD HARRELL
Lyrics by BRAD ARNOLD

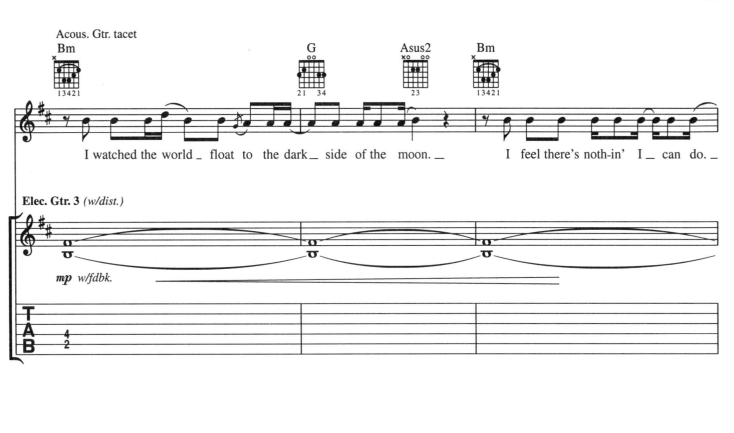

I watched the world _ float to the dark _ side of the moon. _ I feel there's noth-in' I _ can do. _

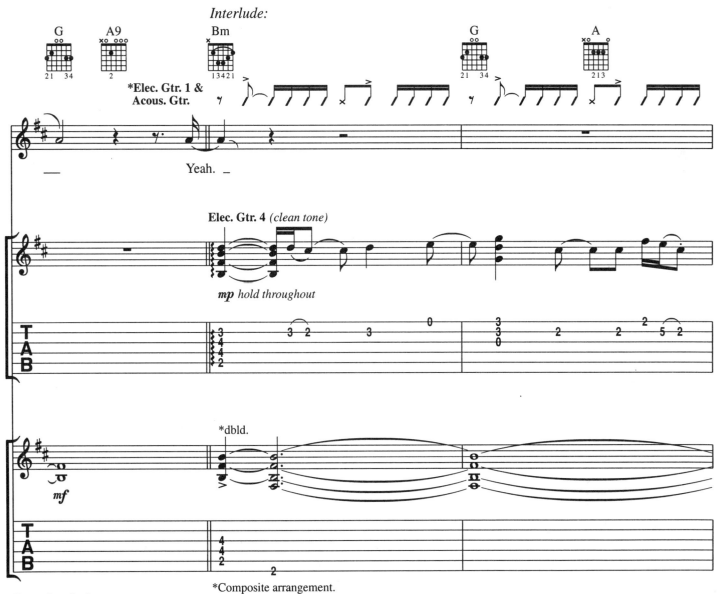

Yeah. _

*Composite arrangement.

Kryptonite – 9 – 2

146

Cont. rhy. simile

Verses 2 & 3:
w/Rhy. Fig. 1 *(Elec. Gtr. 1) 2 times, simile*

2. I watched the world __ float to the dark side of the moon. _____
3. You call me strong, _ you called me weak, but still your se - crets I will

Elec. Gtr. 3 tacet

Af - ter all I knew, it had to be some - thing to do with you. ___
keep. You took for grant - ed all the times I nev - er let you down. _

I real - ly don't mind __ what hap - pens now and then, _ as
You stum - bled in and bumped your head. If not for me, then you'd be

vol. swell w/fdbk.

Kryptonite – 9 – 3

Kryptonite – 9 – 4

Kryp - to - nite. _

Elec. Gtr. 5 *(w/dist.)* on repeat

mf

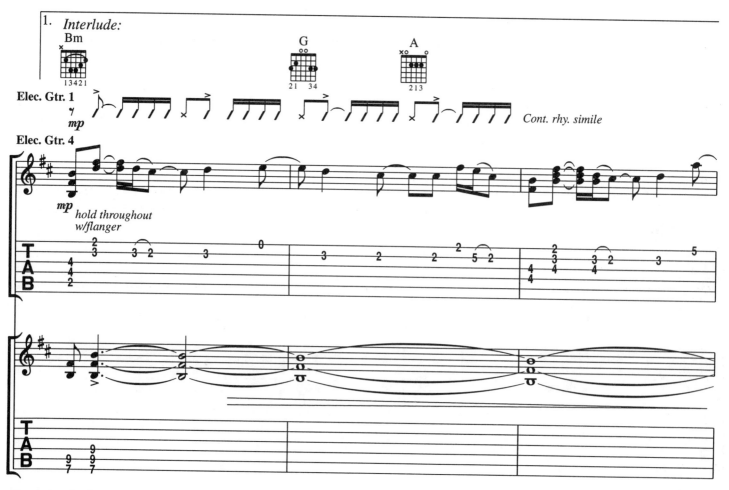

1. *Interlude:*

Elec. Gtr. 1

mp

Cont. rhy. simile

Elec. Gtr. 4

mp
hold throughout
w/flanger

Kryptonite – 9 – 7

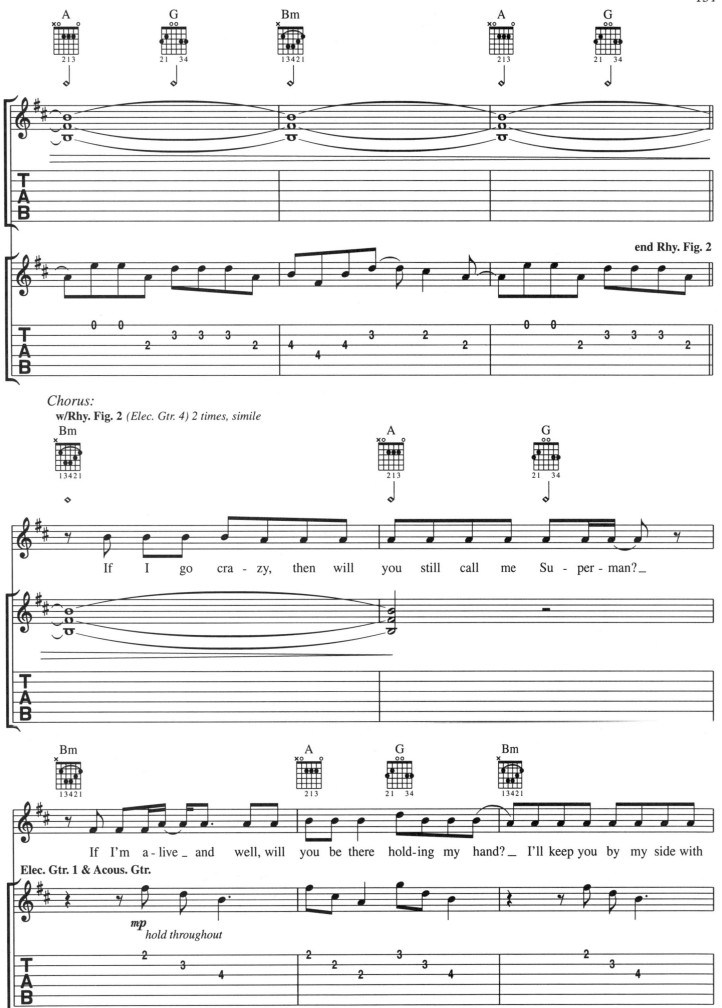

Chorus:

w/Rhy. Fig. 2 *(Elec. Gtr. 4) 2 times, simile*

If I go cra-zy, then will you still call me Su-per-man?

If I'm a-live __ and well, will you be there hold-ing my hand? __ I'll keep you by my side with

Elec. Gtr. 1 & Acous. Gtr.

mp
hold throughout

Kryptonite – 9 – 8

152

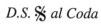

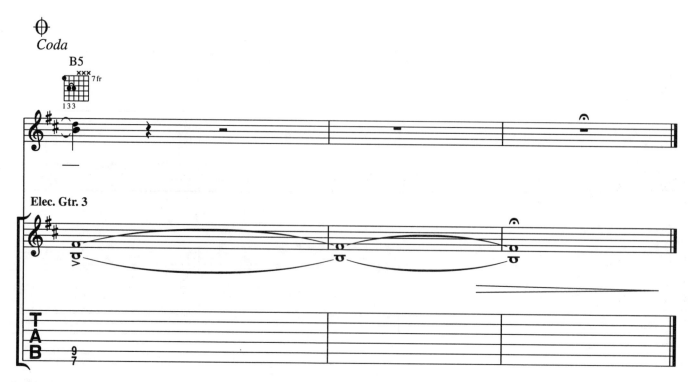

Kryptonite – 9 – 9

MAKE ME BAD

All gtrs. are 7-string gtrs.
tuned down 1 whole step:

⑦= A   ③= F
⑥= D   ②= A
⑤= G   ①= D
④= C

Chord frames for slash notation

B5   C5

*Elec. Gtr. 1 sounds one octave higher (8va) as result of whammy pedal.
**Music sounds a whole step lower than written.

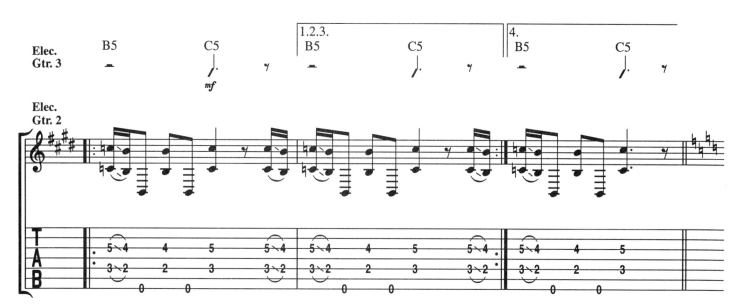

Make Me Bad – 5 – 1

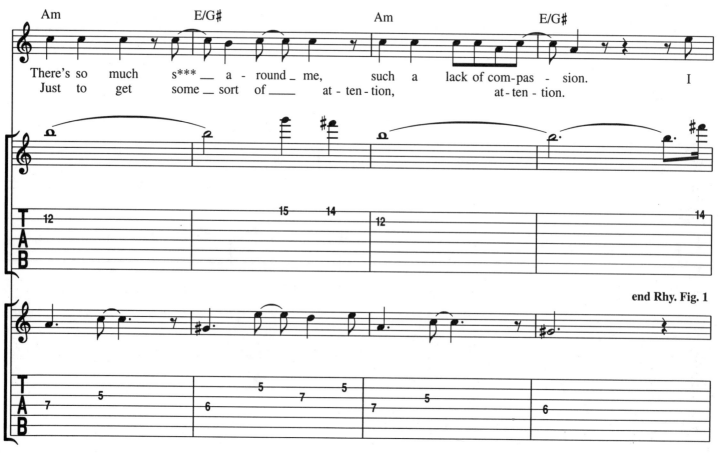

Make Me Bad – 5 – 3

LAST GOODBYE

Words and Music by
KENNY WAYNE SHEPHERD,
MARK SELBY and TIA SILLERS

Elec. Gtrs. 2 & 3/Acous. Gtr. Capo III

Moderately slow ♩ = 78

Intro:

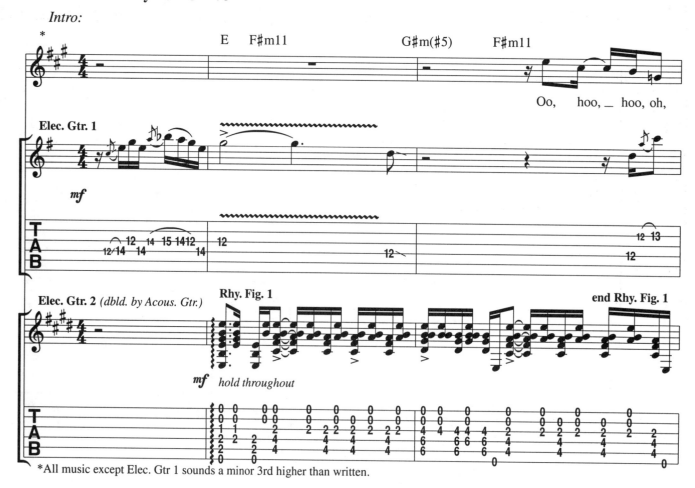

*All music except Elec. Gtr 1 sounds a minor 3rd higher than written.

w/Rhy. Fig. 1 *(Elec. Gtr. 2) simile*

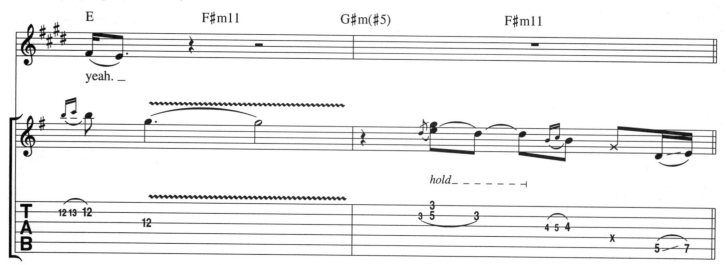

Last Goodbye – 10 – 1

%. *Verse:*

w/Rhy. Fig. 1 *(Elec. Gtr. 1 & Acous. Gtr.) 4 times, simile*

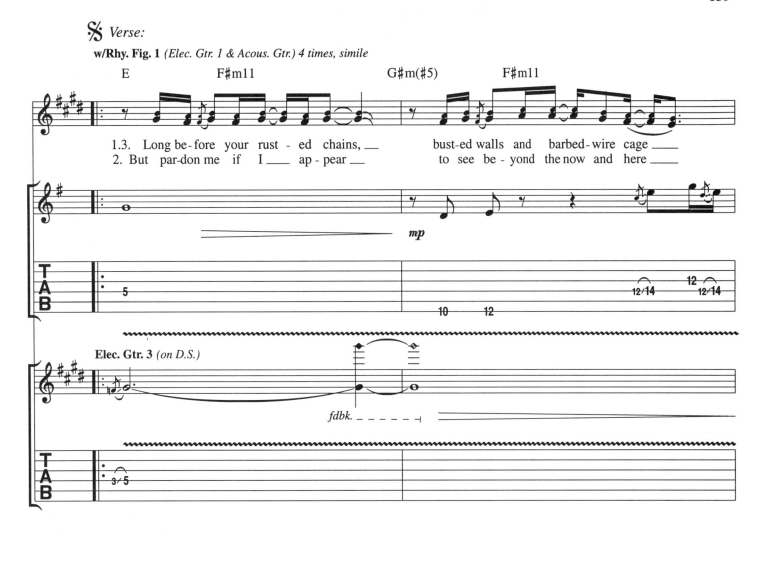

1.3. Long be-fore your rust-ed chains, ___ bust-ed walls and barbed-wire cage ___
2. But par-don me if I ___ ap-pear ___ to see be-yond the now and here ___

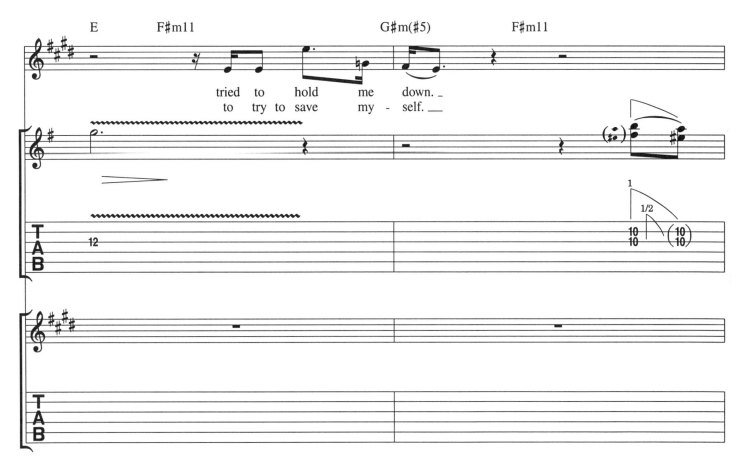

tried to hold me down. ___
to try to save my-self. ___

E   F#m11   G#m(#5)   F#11

And time was just a fist — of change —   tossed — in the wat - er — just in case —

I'm not the kind to pin the blame,   but I can't take more   of the same, —

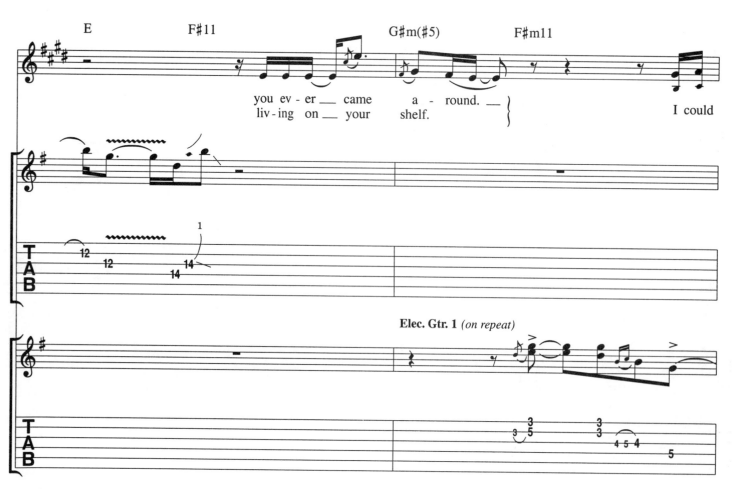

E   F#11   G#m(#5)   F#m11

you ev - er — came   a - round. —   I could

liv - ing on — your   shelf.

Elec. Gtr. 1 *(on repeat)*

Chorus:

lose __ my - self,   I could curse like __ hell. __   But I've

lost   the __ will   to   e - ven __ try. ___   If you

162

Last Goodbye – 10 – 6

164

Bridge:

door clos - es an - oth - er one o - pens. ___ I feel ___ the cold wind blow - in' ___

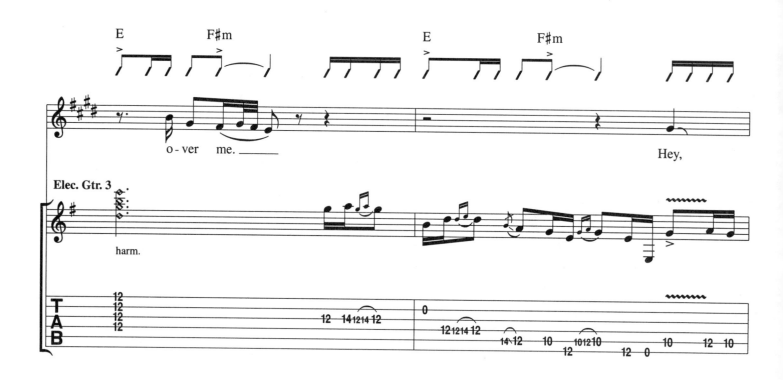

o - ver me. _____ Hey,

harm.

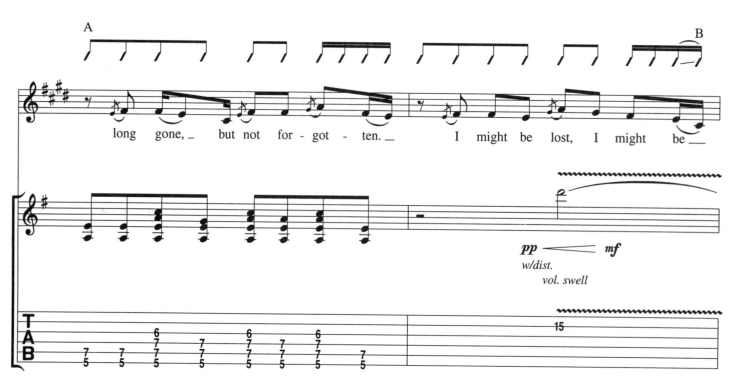

long gone, _ but not for - got - ten. ___ I might be lost, I might be ___

pp ——— *mf*
w/dist.
vol. swell

Last Goodbye – 10 – 7

Guitar Solo:
w/Rhy. Fig. 1 *(Elec. Gtrs. 2 & 3/*
Acous. Gtr.) 3 3/4 times, simile

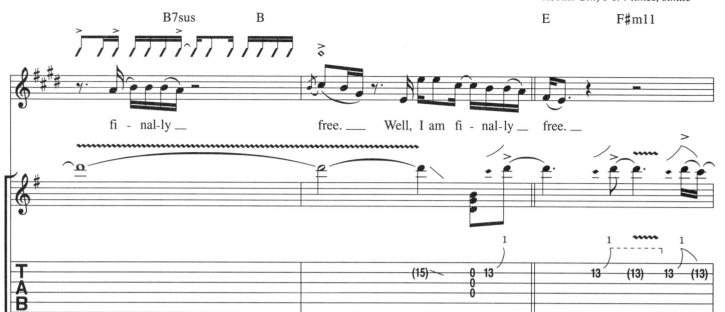

fi - nal-ly ___   free. ___ Well, I am fi - nal-ly ___ free. ___

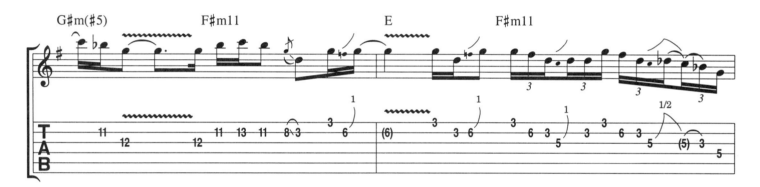

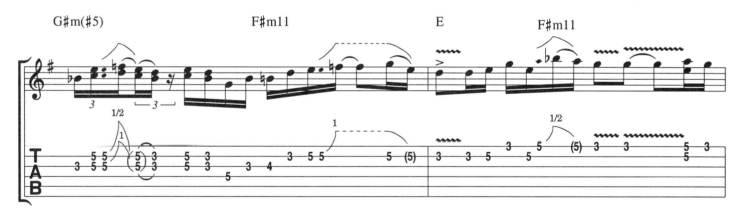

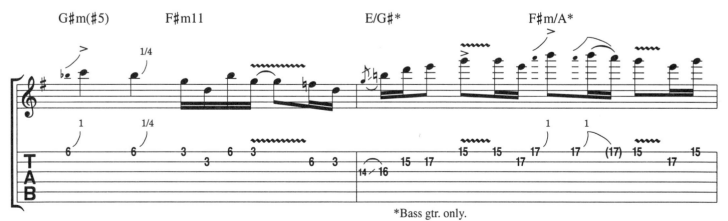

*Bass gtr. only.

Last Goodbye – 10 – 8

166

Last Goodbye – 10 – 9

Yes it is, _____ yes it is. _____

rit. poco a poco

Freely

harm.

Last Goodbye – 10 – 10

LOSER

Music by MATT ROBERTS,
BRAD ARNOLD and TODD HARRELL
Lyrics by BRAD ARNOLD

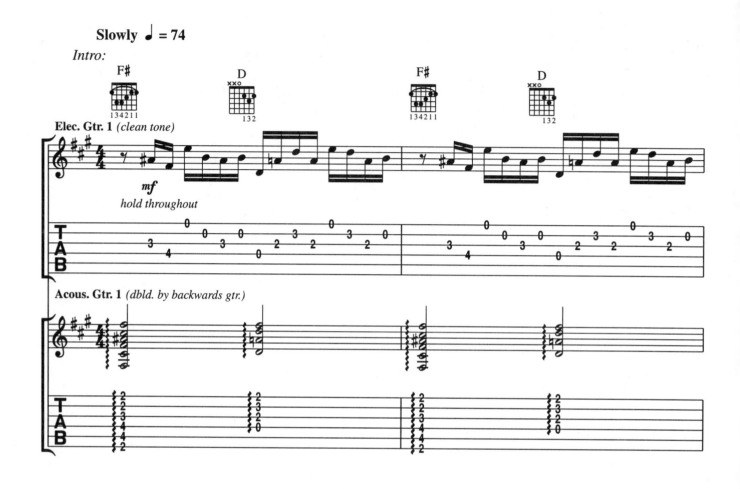

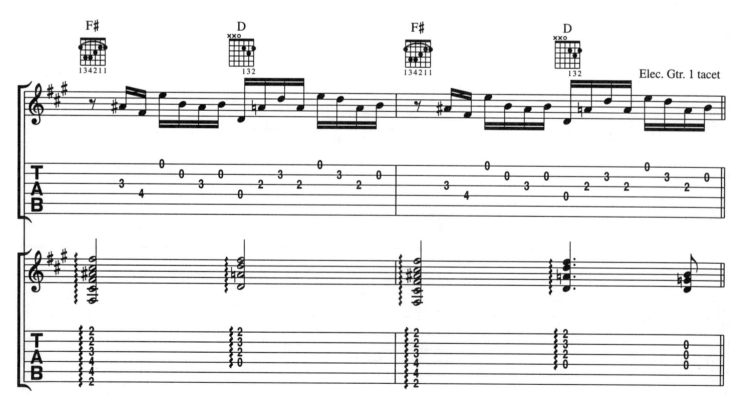

Loser – 8 – 1

Verse:
w/Rhy. Figs. 1 *(Elec. Gtr. 2)* **& 1A** *(Acous. Gtr. 1)1 3/4 times, simile*

1. Breathe in right a - way, _ noth-in' seems _ to fill this _ place. _ I need this ev - 'ry time. _ So
2. This is get-ting old. _ I can't break _ these chains that I hold. My bod-y's grow-in' cold. _ There's

take your lies,___ get off my ___ case. ___ Some-day I will find ___ a
noth-ing left ___ of this mind or my soul. Ad-dic-tion needs a pac-i-fi-er. The

love that flows ___ through me like ___ this. ___ And this will fall ___ a-way. ___
buzz of this poi-son is tak-ing me high-er. And this will fall ___ a-way. ___

𝄋 *Chorus:*

This will fall a-way. ___
This will fall a-way. ___ } You're get-ting clos-er to

push-ing me off ___ of life's ___ lit-tle edge. ___ 'Cause I'm a los-er, the

*Composite arrangement.

172

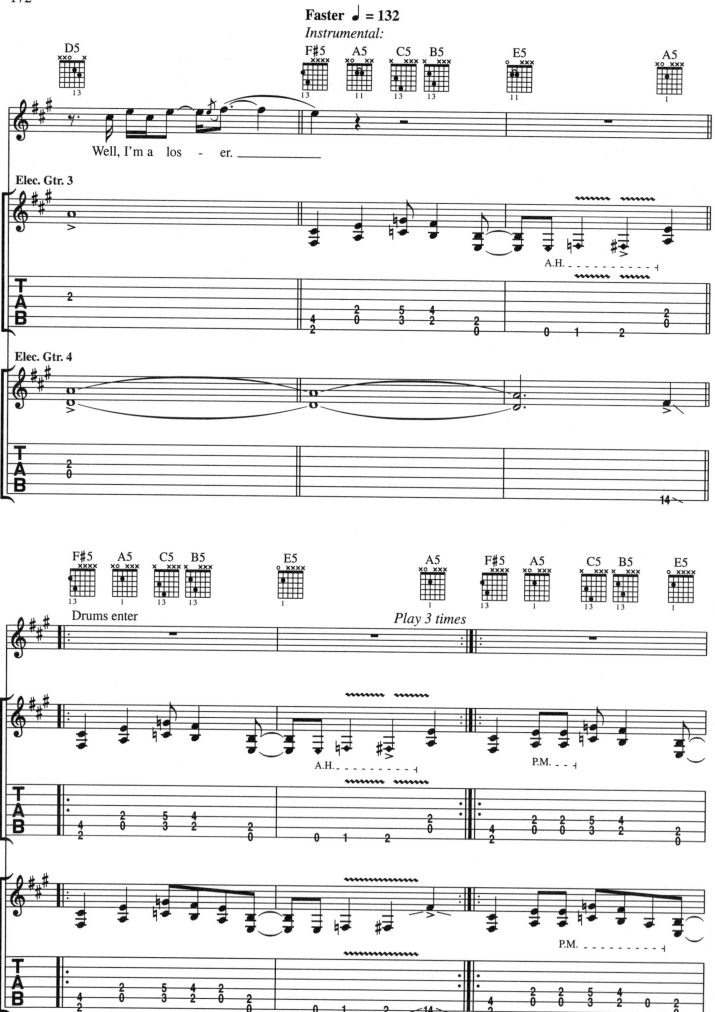

Loser – 8 – 6

Outro Chorus:
w/Vcl. Fig. 1, *simile*
w/Rhy. Fig. 2 *(Elec. Gtrs. 3 & 4) simile*

(Lead vocal:) You're get-ting clos - er to push-in' me off __ of life's _ lit - tle edge. ____

____ Los - er, ba - by. __ The soon - er or lat - er, ____

____ yeah. __ You're hold-ing the rope _ and I'm tak - in', ____ I'm tak-

Elec. Gtr. 5 *(w/dist.)*
mp

- in', ___ I'm tak - in'. __ Yeah. ____

Elec. Gtrs. 3 & 4

Loser – 8 – 8

MARIA MARIA

Words and Music by
WYCLEF JEAN, JERRY DUPLESSIS,
CARLOS SANTANA, KARL PERAZZO and RAUL REKOW

Lyrics:

La - dies _ and gents, _

turn up _ your sound _ sys - tem _ to the sound of Car - los San - ta - na and the G and B Pro - duct.

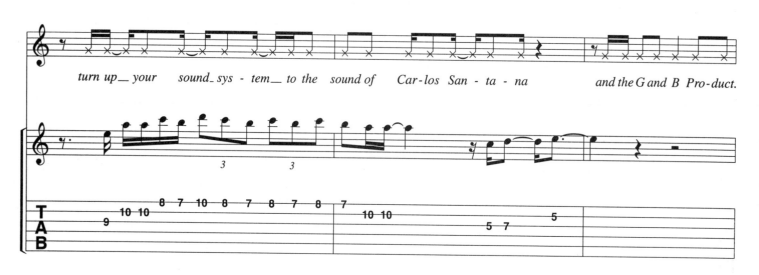

180

Maria Maria - 16 - 5

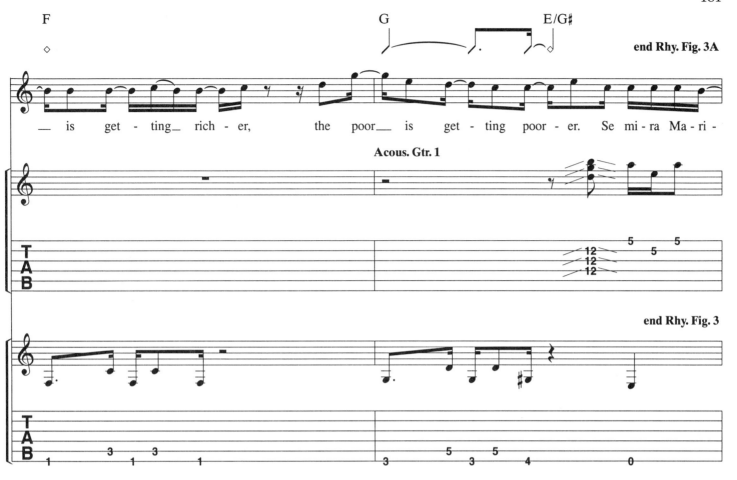

end Rhy. Fig. 3A

Acous. Gtr. 1

end Rhy. Fig. 3

___ is get - ting___ rich - er, the poor___ is get - ting poor - er. Se mi - ra Ma - ri -

w/Rhy. Figs. 3 *(Bass)* & 3A *(Keybd.) simile*

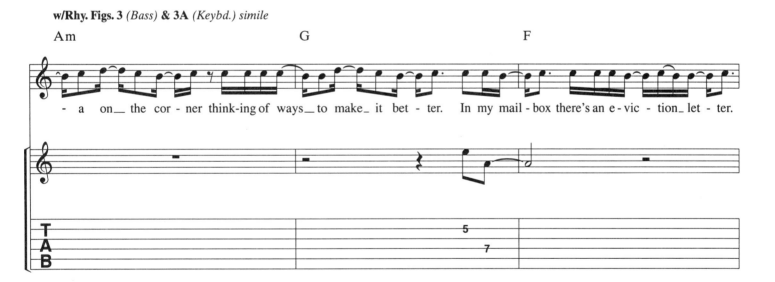

- a on___ the cor - ner think-ing of ways___ to make___ it bet - ter. In my mail - box there's an e - vic - tion___ let - ter.

w/Rhy. Fig. 1 *(Bass) 2 times, simile*

Vocal Fig. 1

Some-bod - y just___ said see___ you lat - er. Yeah._____

Bkgd. vcl.: A - ho - ra ven - go ma-ma cho-la, ma-ma cho-la. A -

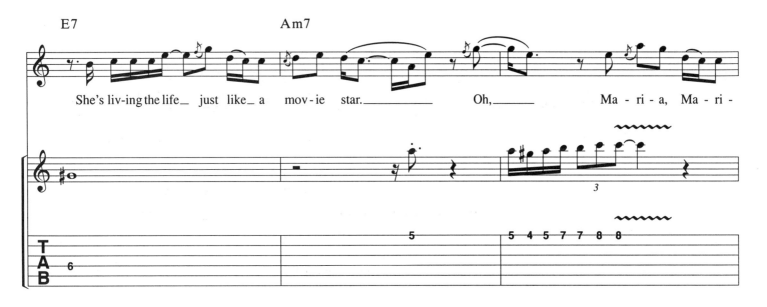

w//Rhy. Fig. 1 *(Bass) 2 times, simile*

Am

- na.

Elec. Gtr. 1

Verse 2:

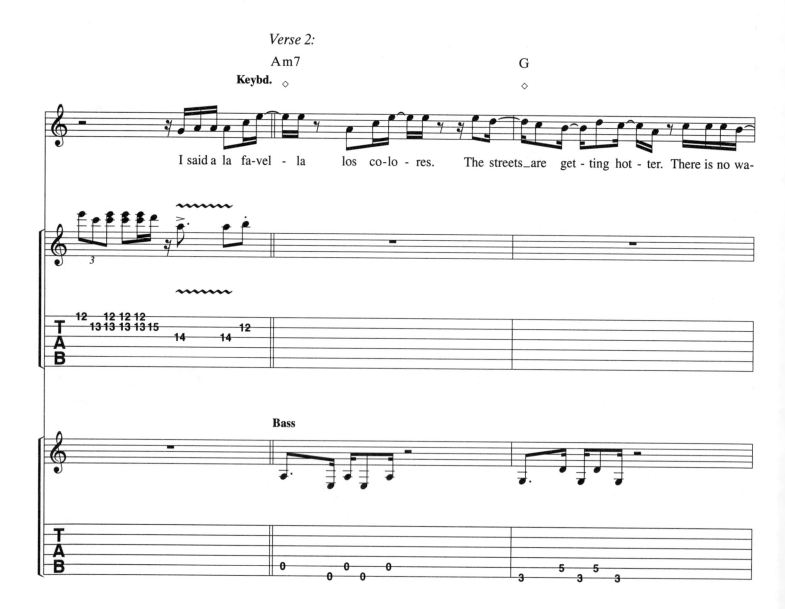

Am7   G

Keybd.

I said a la fa-vel - la   los co-lo - res.   The streets are get - ting hot - ter. There is no wa-

Bass

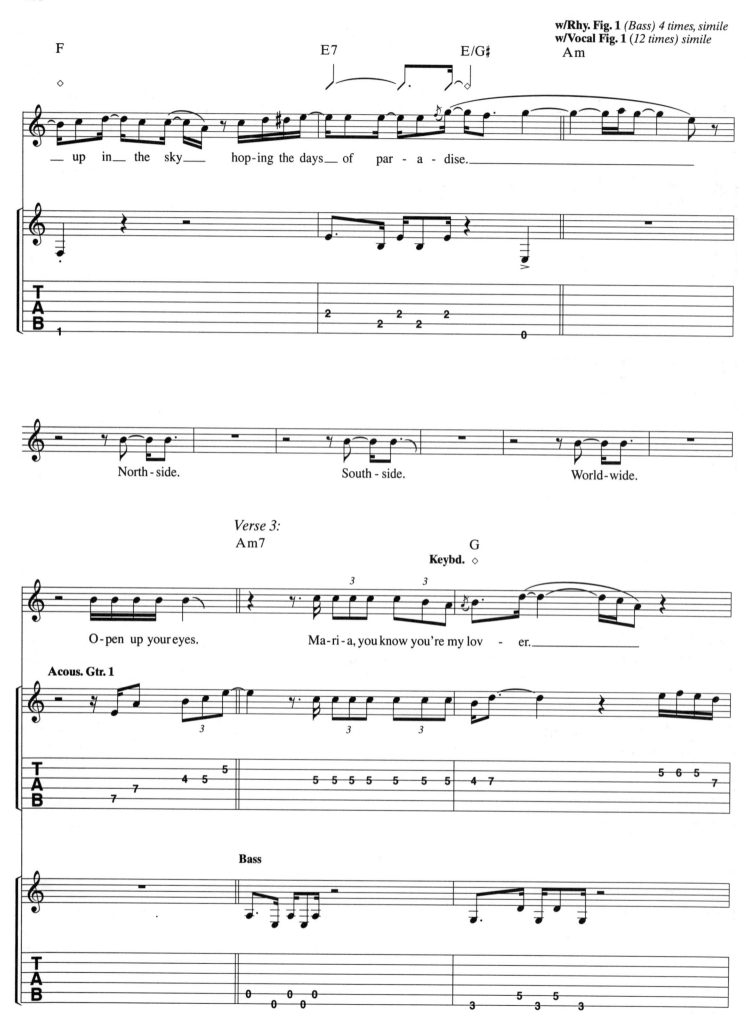

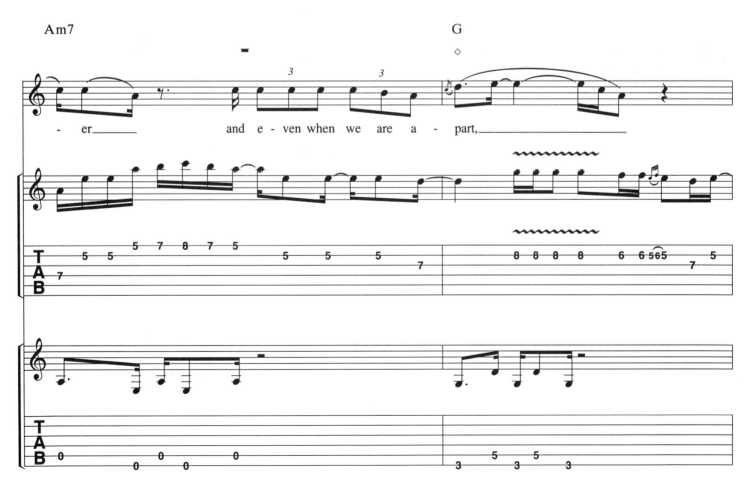

188

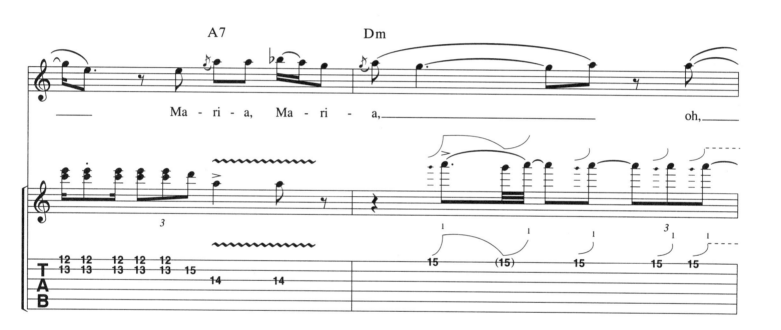

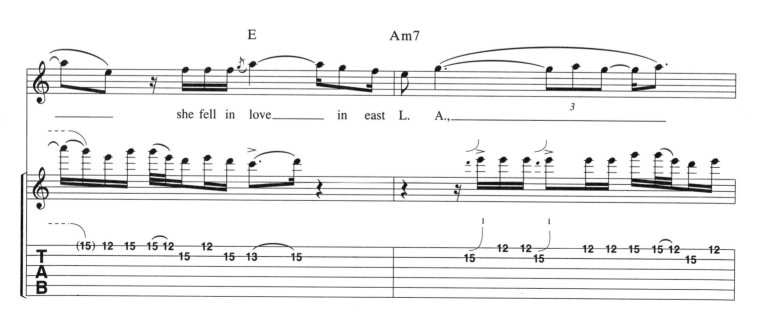

Slow fade

Fade

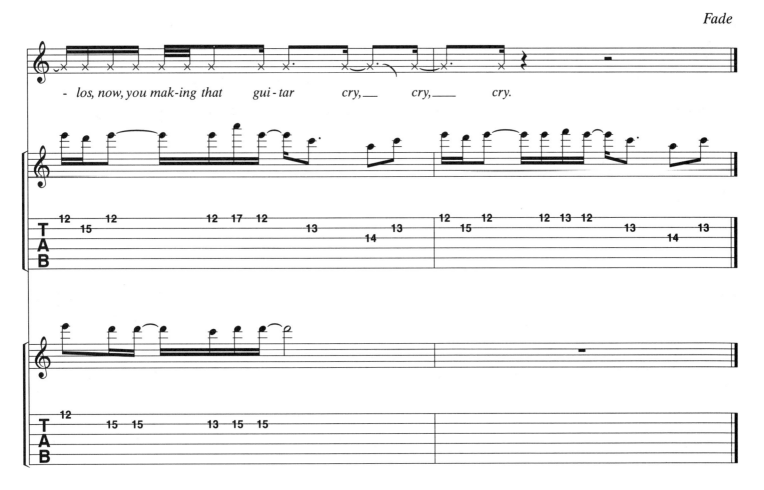

MINORITY

Lyrics by BILLIE JOE
Music by GREEN DAY

Minority - 4 - 1

193

Minority - 4 - 2

194

Minority - 4 - 3

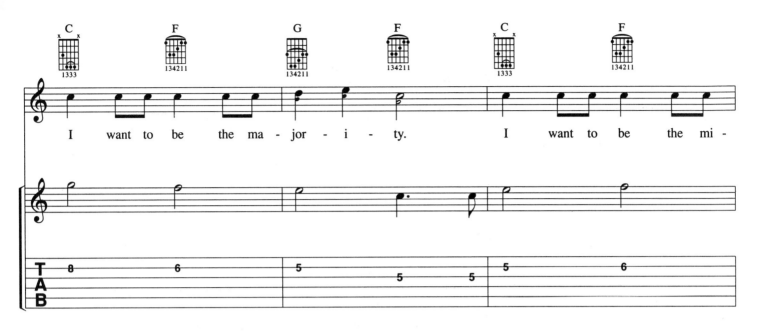

I want to be the ma - jor - i - ty. I want to be the mi -

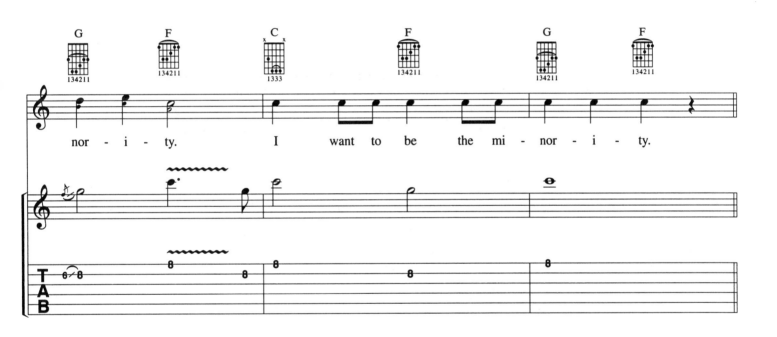

nor - i - ty. I want to be the mi - nor - i - ty.

Outro:
w/Rhy. Fig. 1 *(Acous. Gtr.)* Elec. Gtr. 1 tacet *rit.*

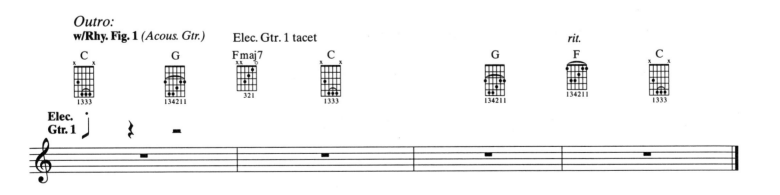

Elec. Gtr. 1

MUDSHOVEL

All gtrs. tuned:
⑥ = A♭   ③ = D♭
⑤ = D♭   ② = G♭
④ = A♭   ① = B♭

Words and Music by
MICHAEL MUSHOK, AARON LEWIS,
JOHN APRIL and JONATHAN WYSOCKI

Moderate rock ♩ = 108

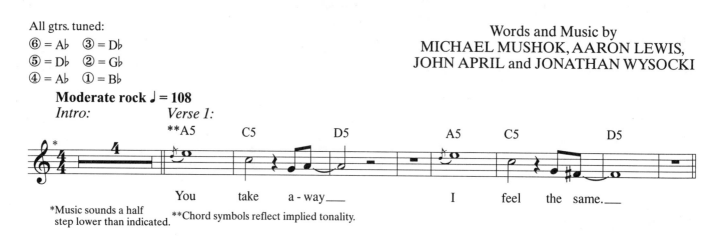

*Music sounds a half step lower than indicated.   **Chord symbols reflect implied tonality.

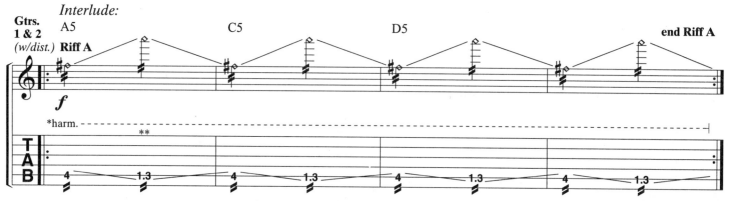

*Random harmonics are sounded by lightly touching ⑤ str. and sliding as indicated, while picking in 16th-note rhythm (♫♫).
**Harmonic is located between 1st & 2nd frets.

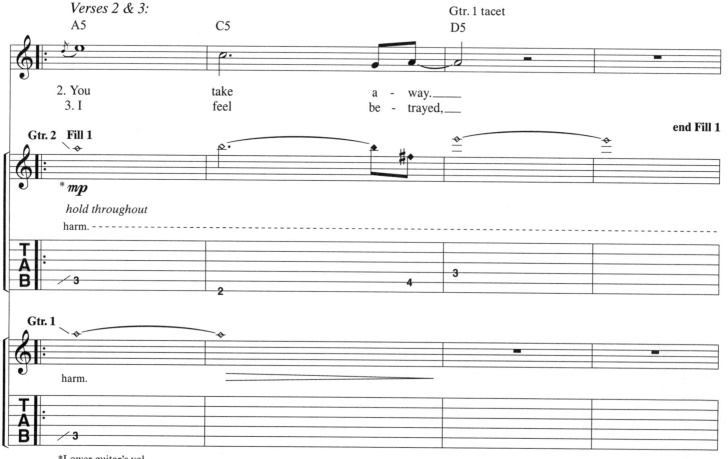

*Lower guitar's vol.

Mudshovel - 5 - 2

200

Mudshovel - 5 - 5

NO WAY OUT

Words and Music by
DEAN DELEO, ROBERT DELEO,
ERIC KRETZ and SCOTT WEILAND

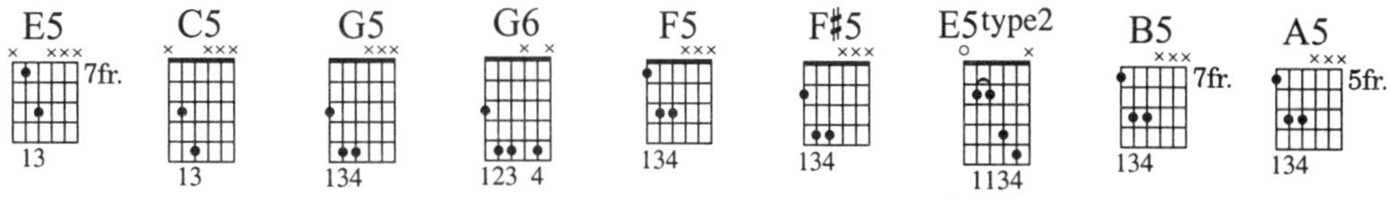

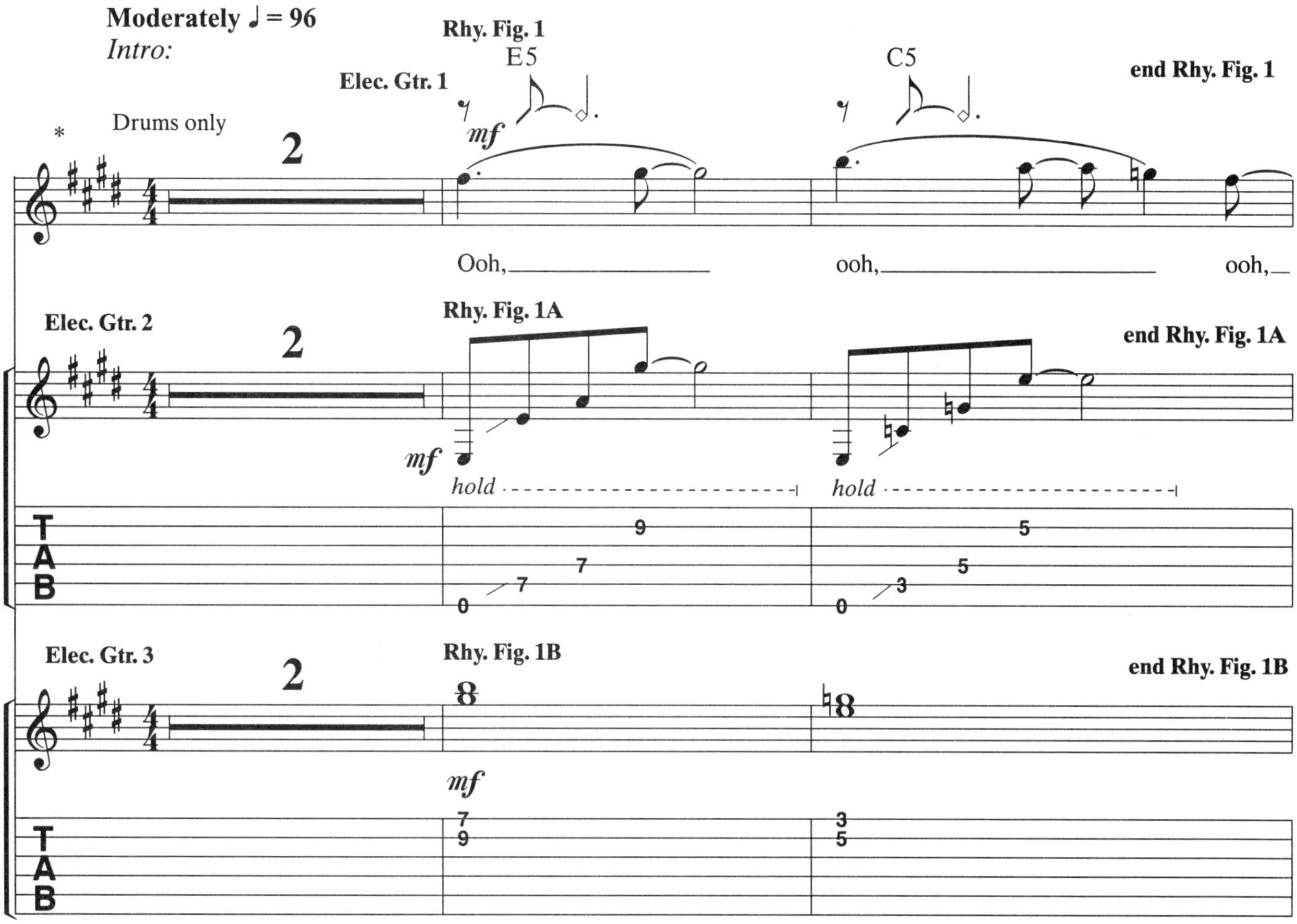

All gtrs. tune down 2 whole steps:

⑥ = C   ③ = E♭
⑤ = F   ② = G
④ = B♭ ① = C

*Music sounds two whole steps lower than written.

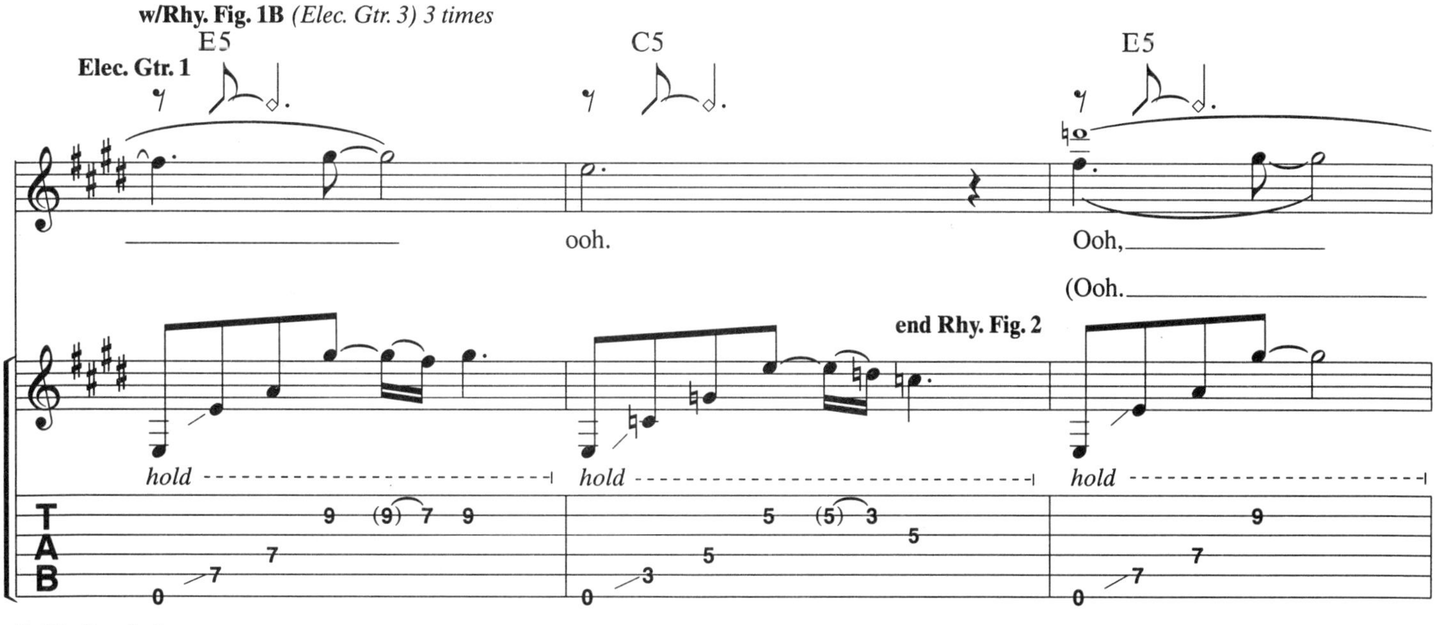

drown-ing but__ I'm hold-ing__ on.__   What keeps me breath-ing?__

Don't have an an-swer,__ I'm drown-ing but__ I won't let__ go.__

%Chorus:

A - way now._____

*Bkgd. vcls. second time only.

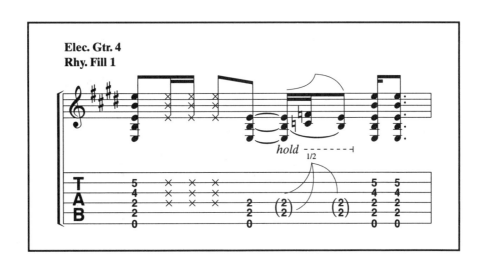

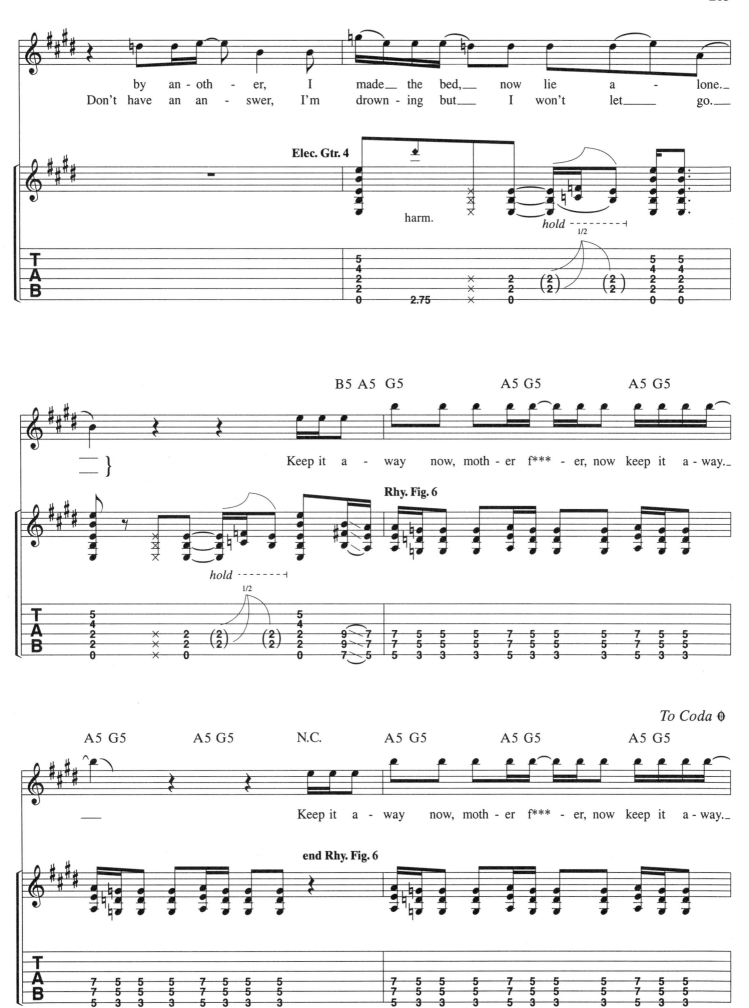

206

No Way Out - 9 - 6

Way now, moth - er f*** - er, now keep it a - way.___

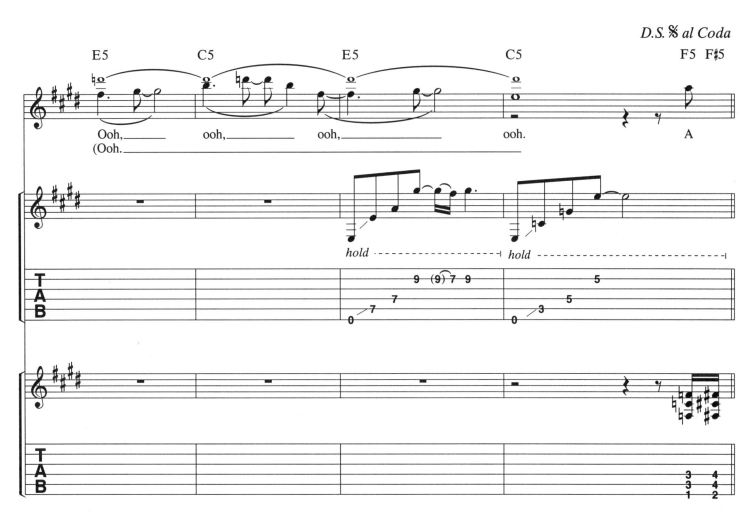

D.S. % al Coda

Ooh,_____ ooh,_____ ooh,_____ ooh. A
(Ooh._____

hold - - - - - - - - - - - *hold* -

Rhy. Fig. 7

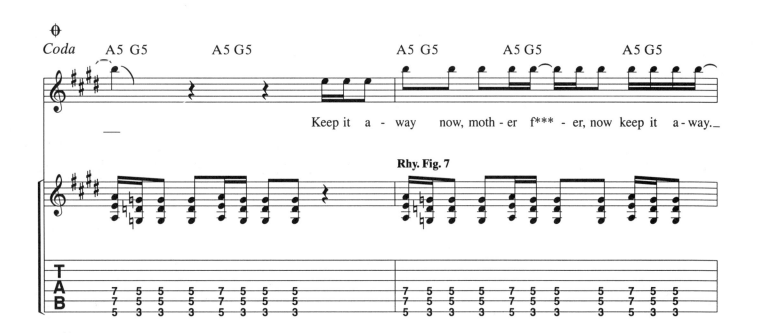

Coda

Keep it a - way now, moth - er f*** - er, now keep it a - way.__

No Way Out - 9 - 7

208

MY FAVORITE HEADACHE

Lyrics by GEDDY LEE
Music by GEDDY LEE and BEN MINK

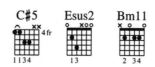

Moderately fast ♩ = 124

Intro:

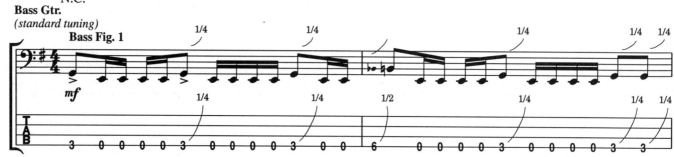

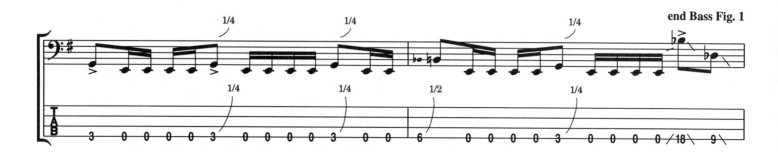

My Favorite Headache – 10 – 1

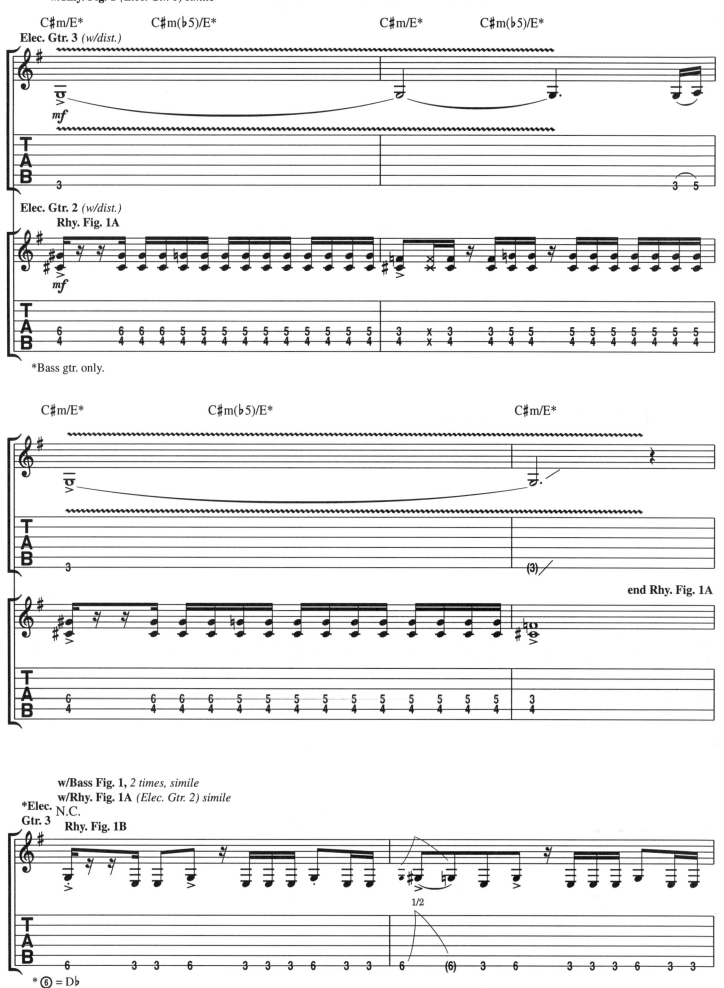

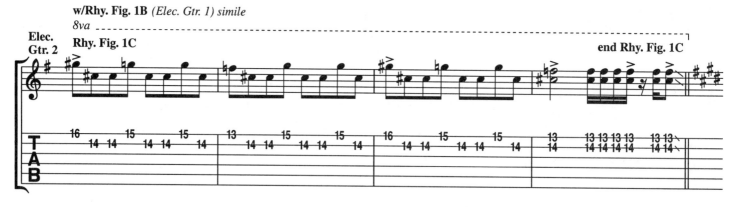

Verse 1:

One man stand-ing on the plains of A - bra-ham, watch-ing the dam - aged sun - rise. ___

One man stand-ing near the edge of a qui-et break - down. ___

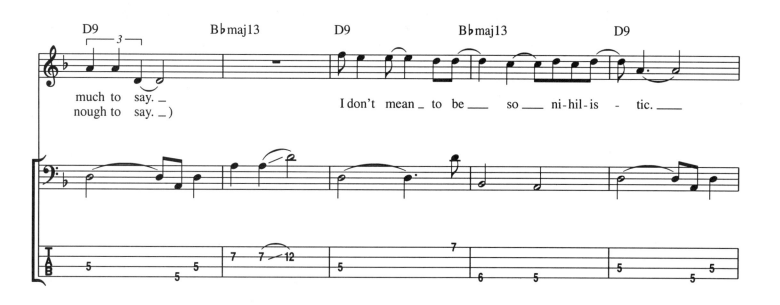

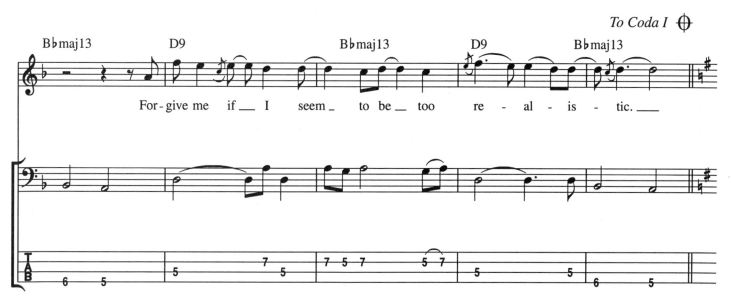

216

My Favorite Headache – 10 – 7

218

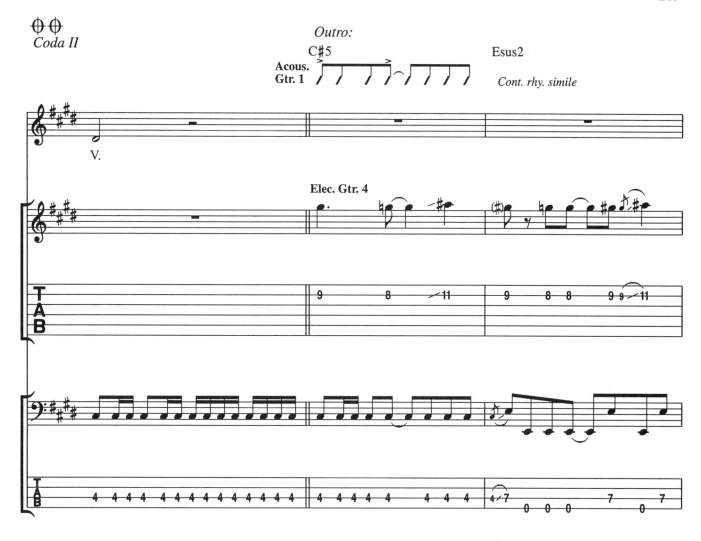

My Favorite Headache – 10 – 10

NOOKIE

*Tuning (all gtrs.):
⑥=F♯ ③=E
⑤=F♯ ②=omit
④=B   ①=omit

Lyrics by Fred Durst
Music by Wes Borland, Sam Rivers,
John Otto and Leor Dimant

Moderately slow rock ♩ = 98
Intro:

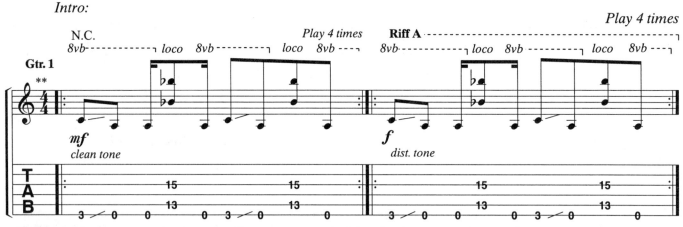

*Wes Borland uses a custom 4-string guitar. You can use a standard 6- or 7-string, remove the top strings,
and tune the bottom 4 strings as indicated using heavy gauge strings (the 6th is a .65 bass string).
**Music sounds a minor 3rd lower than written.

Nookie - 6 - 1

Hey,— I think a-bout the day
(Days.)
my girl-ie ran a-way with my pay when fel-las came to

w/Fill 1 *(Gtr. 2)*
1.
play. Now she's stuck with my hom-ies that she f***ed, and I'm just a suck-er with a lump in my
(Play.) (Ooh.)

Gtr. 1
Rhy. Fill 1
8vb *loco* *8vb* *loco*

T A B

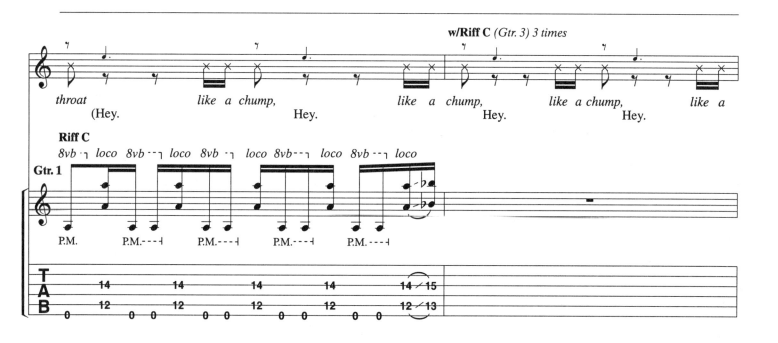

w/Riff C *(Gtr. 3) 3 times*

throat like a chump, like a chump, like a chump, like a
(Hey. Hey. Hey. Hey.

Riff C
8vb *loco* *8vb* *loco* *8vb* *loco* *8vb* *loco* *8vb* *loco*
Gtr. 1
P.M. P.M. P.M. P.M. P.M.

T A B

chump, like a chump, like a chump, like a chump. **2.** Should I be
Hey. Hey. Hey. Hey.)

222

Nookie - 6 - 3

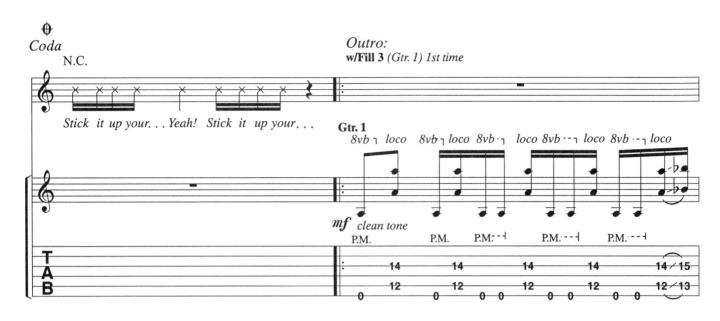

Coda

Outro:
w/**Fill 3** *(Gtr. 1) 1st time*

Stick it up your... Yeah! Stick it up your...

Repeat and fade

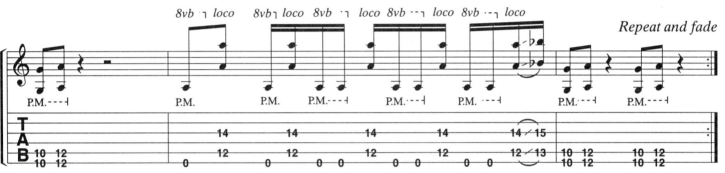

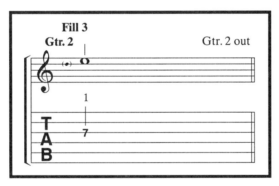

Verse 2:
Should I be feelin' bad? (No.) Should I be feelin' good? (No.)
It's kinda sad, I'm the laughin' stock of the neighborhood.
And you would think that I'd be movin' on, (Movin'.)
But I'm a sucker like I said, f***-up in the head. (Not.)
Maybe she just made a mistake and I should give her a break.
My heart'll ache either way.
Hey, what the hell. What you want me to say?
I won't lie that I can't deny.
(To Chorus:)

Verse 3:
Why did it take so long?
Why did I wait so long, huh, to figure it out?
But I didn't.
And I'm the only one underneath the sun who didn't get it.
I can't believe that I could be deceived (But you were.) by my so-called girl,
But in reality had a hidden agenda.
She put my tender heart in a blender,
And still I surrendered
(Hey.) like a chump, etc.
(To Chorus:)

ONLY GOD KNOWS WHY

Words and Music by
ROBERT "KID ROCK" RITCHIE,
MATTHEW SHAFER and JOHN TRAVIS

Only God Knows Why – 8 – 1

230

Only God Knows Why – 8 – 5

Only God Knows Why – 8 – 6

232

Only God Knows Why – 8 – 7

233

riv - er._____ Hey, __ hey, _____ hey. _____

Outro:

Elec. Gtr. 2 &
Acous. Gtr.

Elec. Gtr. 1

Verse 4:
People don't know about the things I say and do.
They don't understand about the s*** that I've been through.
It's been so long since I've been home.
I've been gone. . . I've been gone for way too long.

Verse 5:
Maybe I forgot all things I miss.
Oh, somehow, I know there's more to life than this.
I said it too many times
And I still stand firm:
You get what you put in
And people get what they deserve.

Only God Knows Why – 8 – 8

PUT YOUR LIGHTS ON

Words and Music by
ERIK SCHRODY

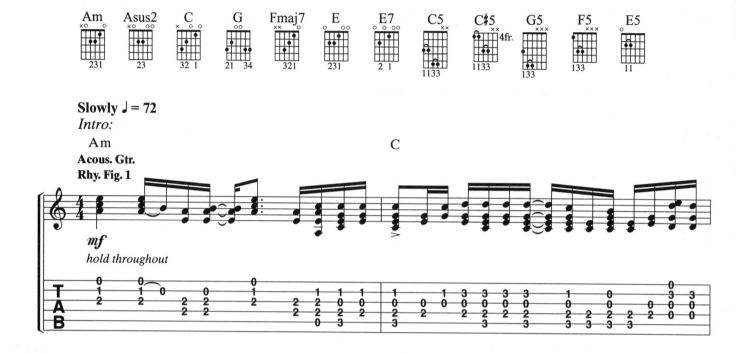

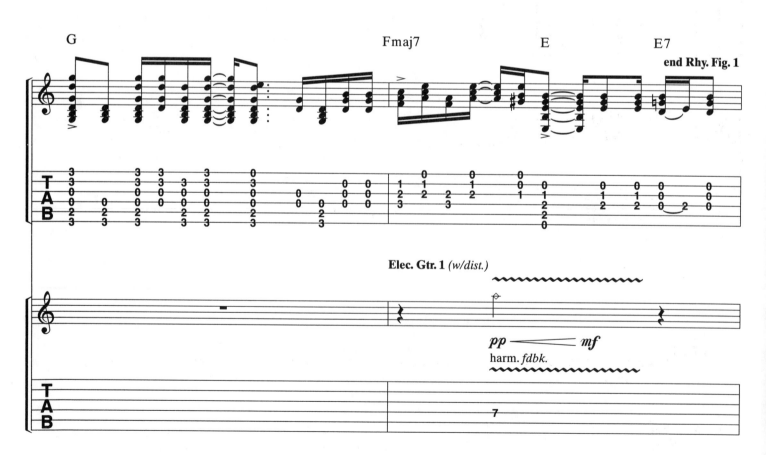

Put Your Lights On - 12 - 1

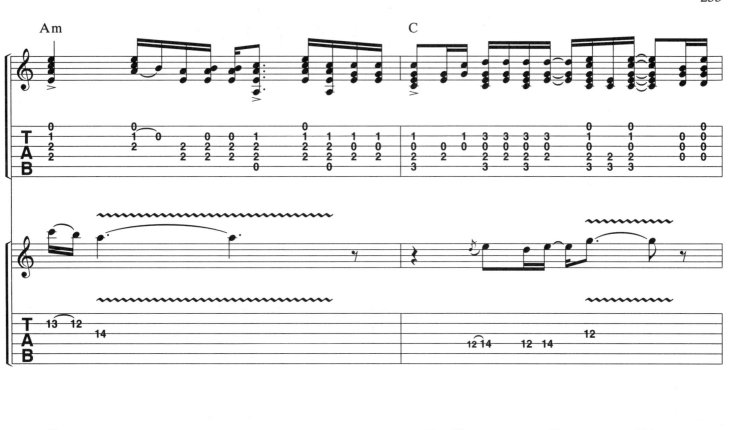

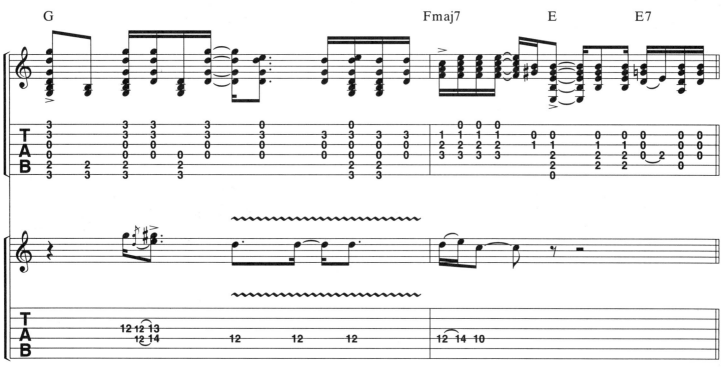

Chorus:

Hey now,   all you sin - ners,____   put your lights_ on,_____

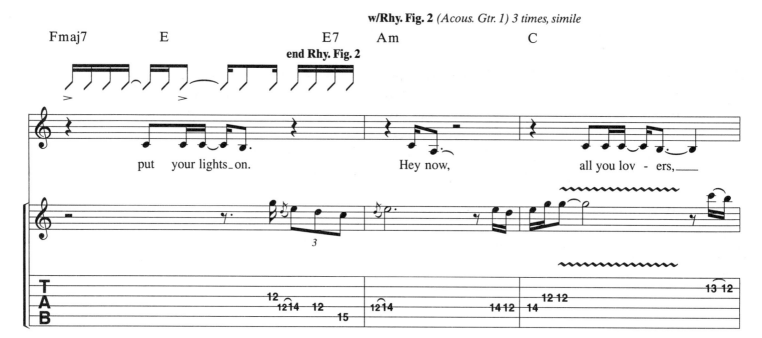

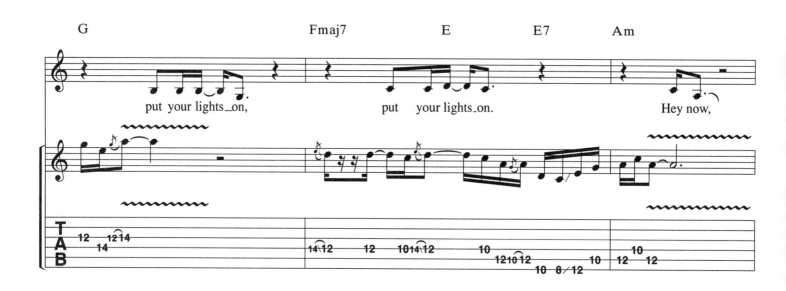

Verse 1:

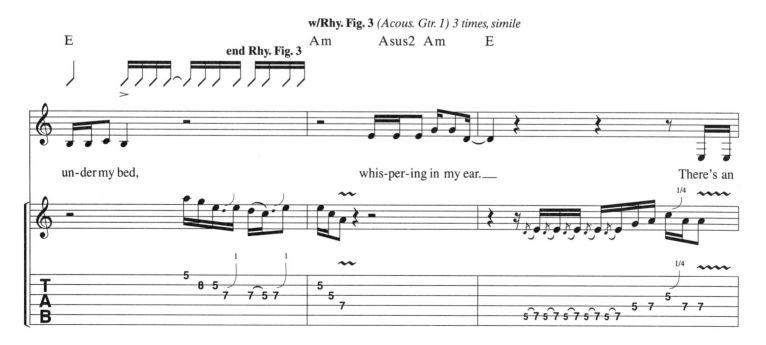

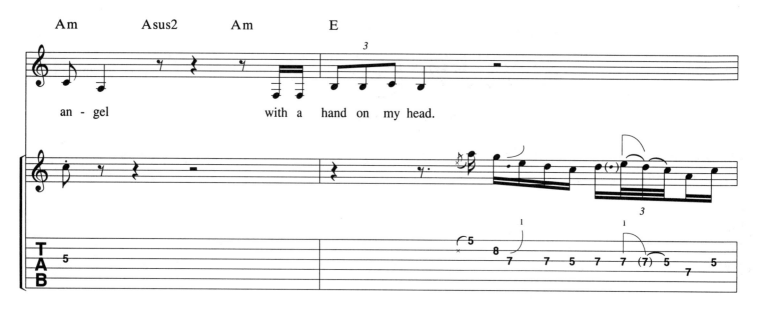

an - gel   with a hand on my head.

She say I got noth-ing to fear.___   There's a

Verse 2:
w/Rhy. Fig. 3 *(Acous. Gtr. 1) 4 times, simile*

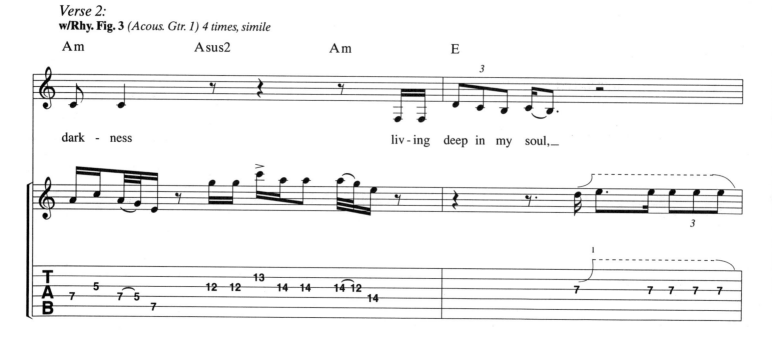

dark - ness   liv - ing deep in my soul,___

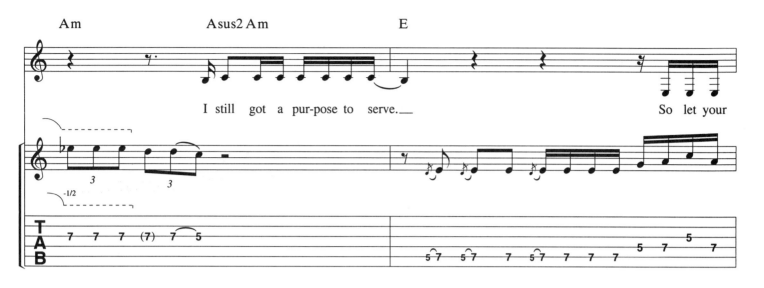

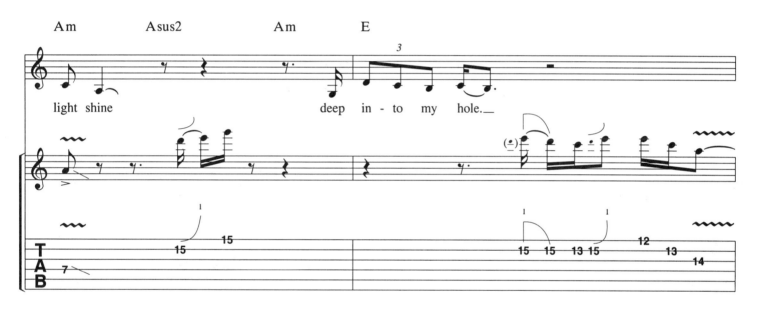

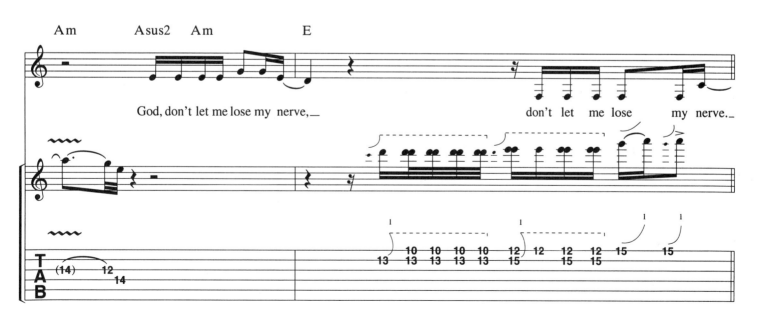

240

Guitar Solo:

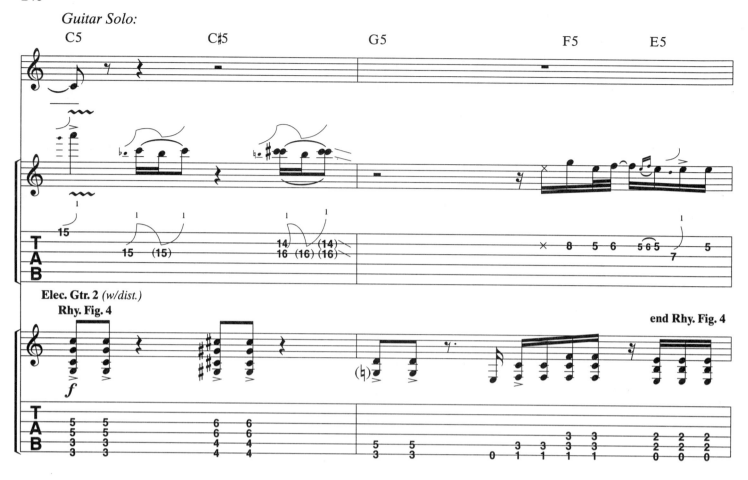

Elec. Gtr. 2 *(w/dist.)*

Rhy. Fig. 4

end Rhy. Fig. 4

w/Rhy. Fig. 4 (Elec. Gtr. 2) 3 times, simile

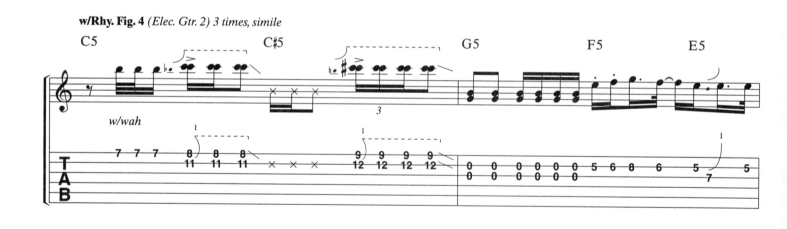

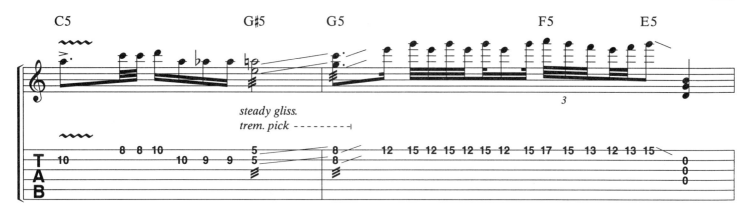

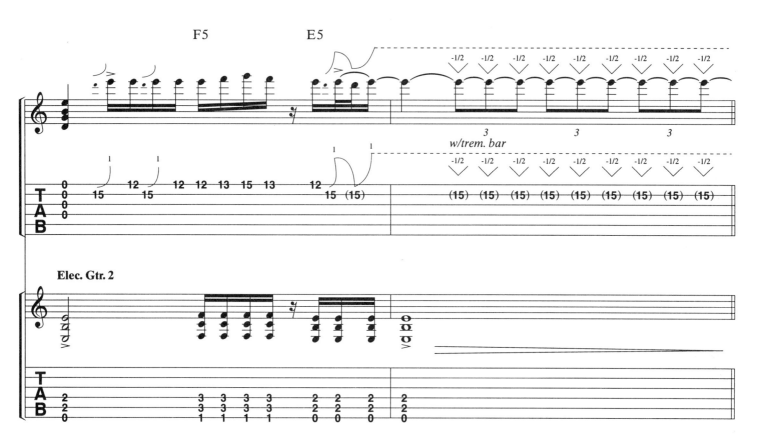

w//Rhy. Fig. 1 *(Acous. Gtr.)* 2 times, simile

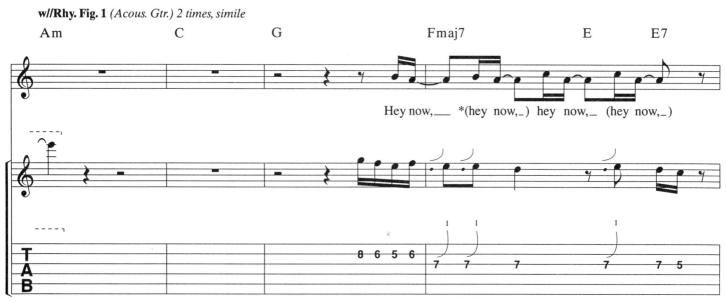

Hey now,___ *(hey now,_) hey now,_ (hey now,_)

*Echo repeats in parenthesis.

Chorus:
w/Rhy. Fig. 2 *(Acous. Gtr.) 2 times, simile*

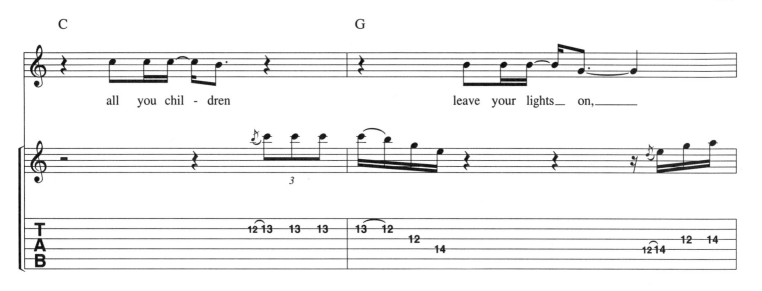

all you chil - dren   leave your lights_ on,_____

Verse 3:
w/Rhy. Fig. 3 *(Acous. Gtr.) 4 times, simile*

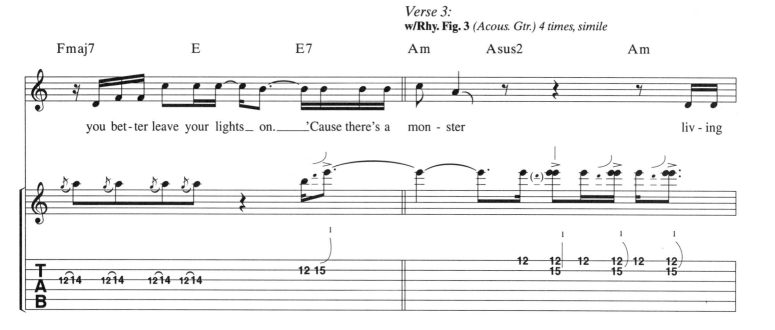

you bet - ter leave your lights_ on._____ 'Cause there's a mon - ster   liv - ing

un - der my bed   whis - per - ing in my ear._

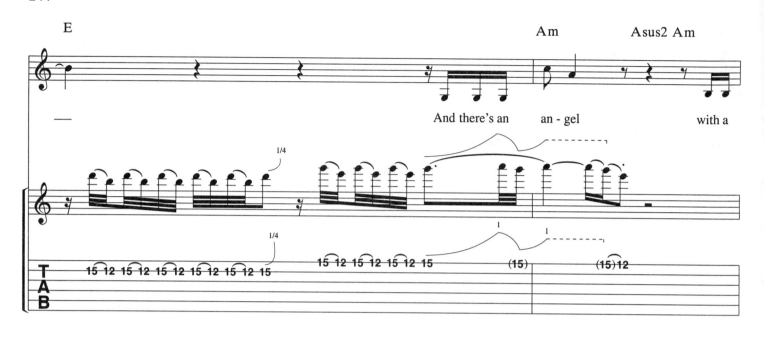

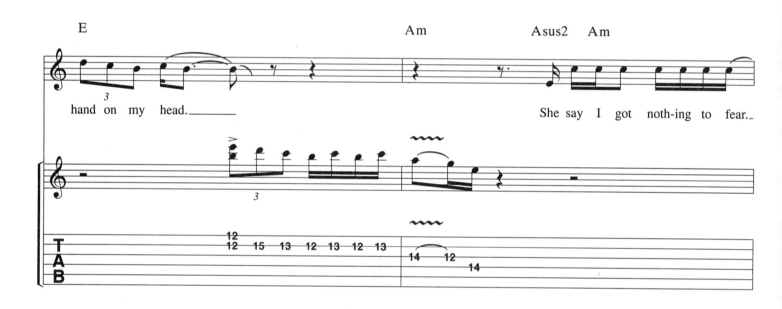

Outro:
w/Rhy. Fig. 1 *(Acous. Gtr.) 2 times, simile*

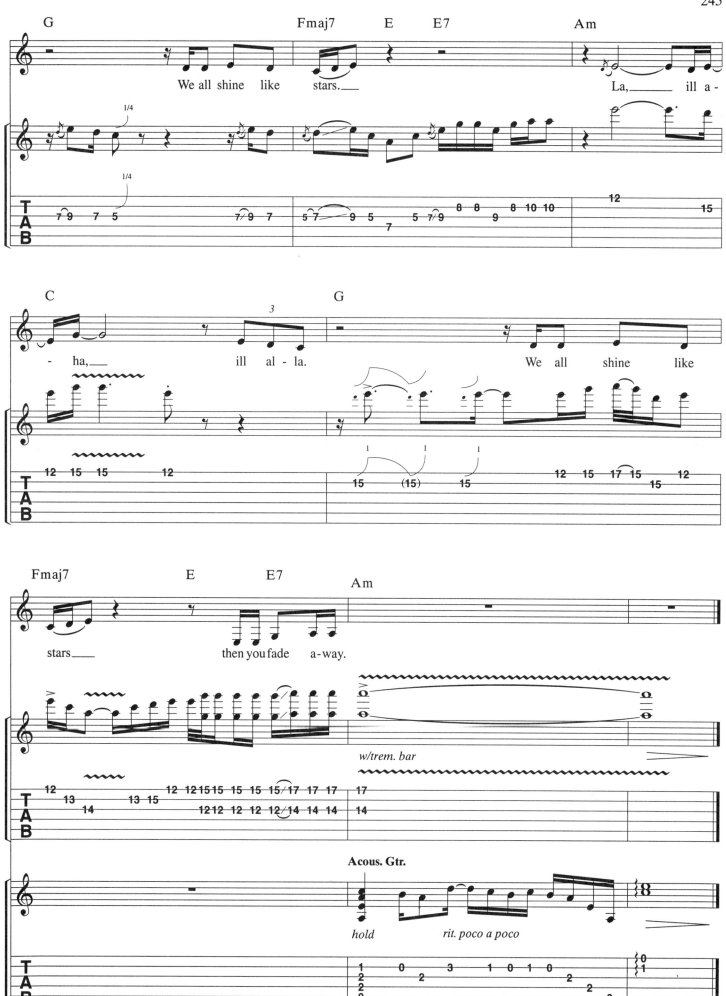

RE-ARRANGED

Lyrics by Fred Durst
Music by Wes Borland, Sam Rivers,
John Otto and Leor Dimant

Re-arranged - 9 - 1

Re-arranged - 9 - 2

248

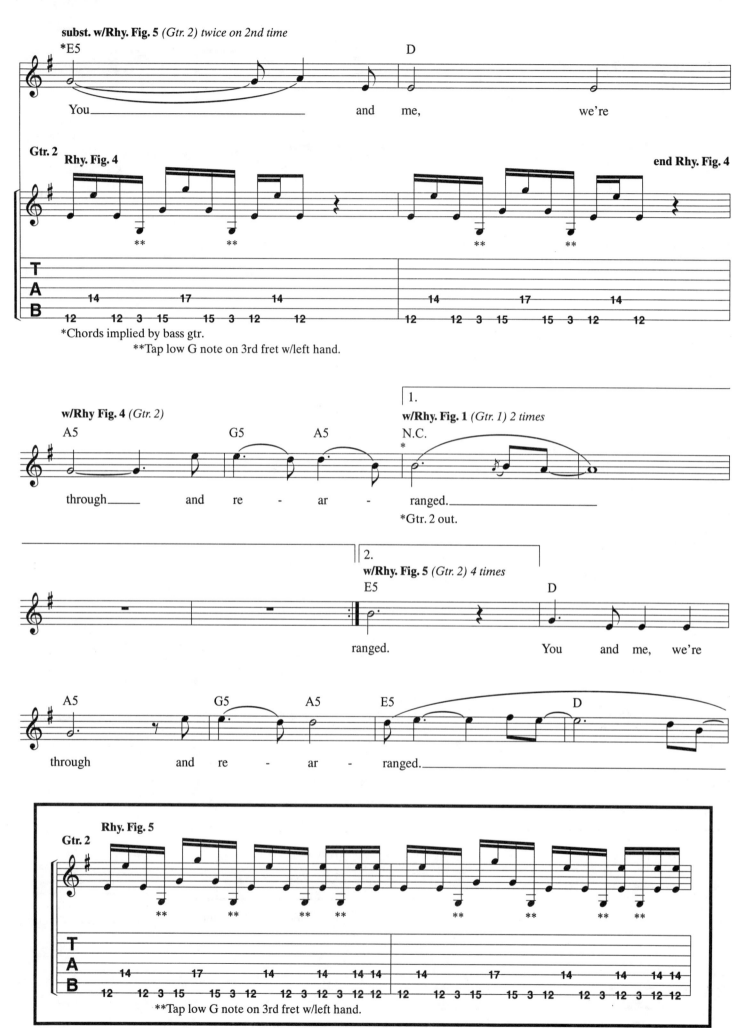

*Chords implied by bass gtr.

**Tap low G note on 3rd fret w/left hand.

**Tap low G note on 3rd fret w/left hand.

Re-arranged - 9 - 4

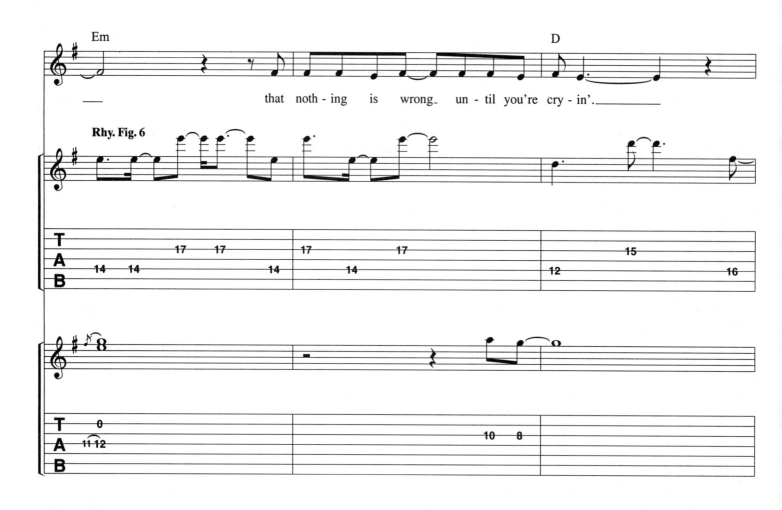

that noth - ing is wrong___ un - til you're cry - in'._____

Rhy. Fig. 6

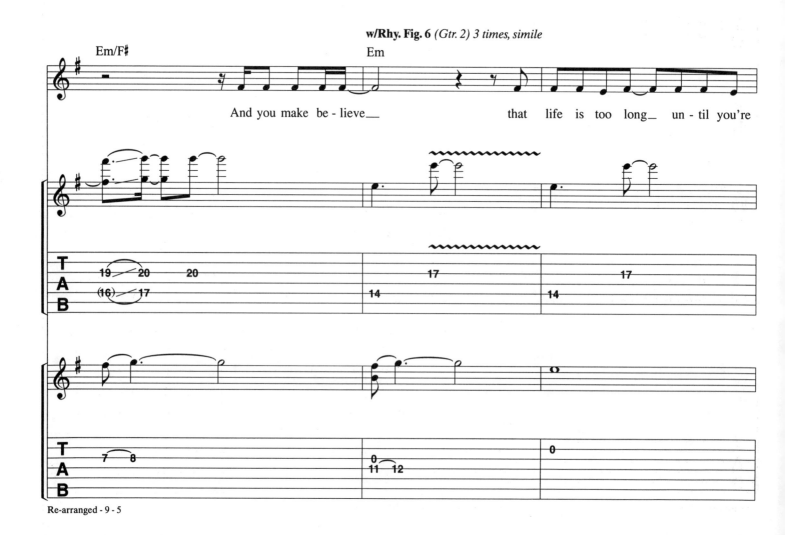

w/Rhy. Fig. 6 *(Gtr. 2) 3 times, simile*

And you make be - lieve___   that   life is too long___ un - til you're

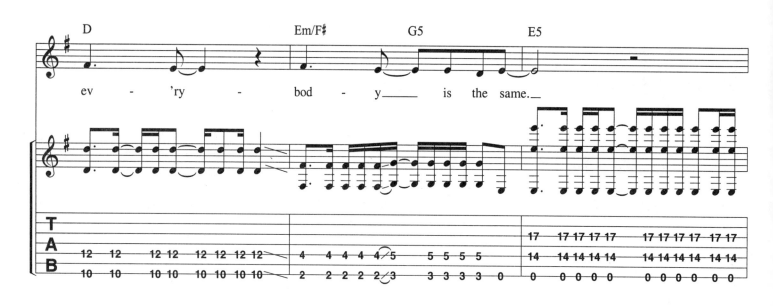

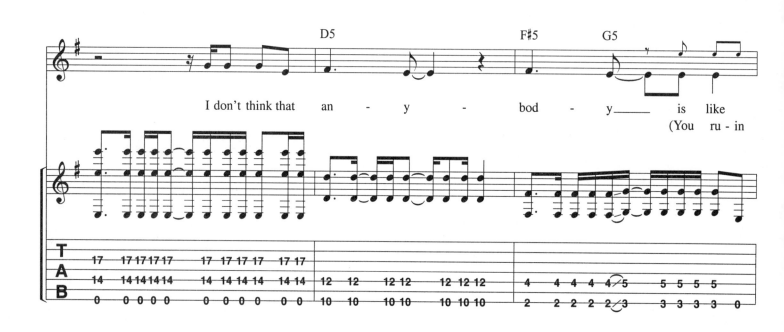

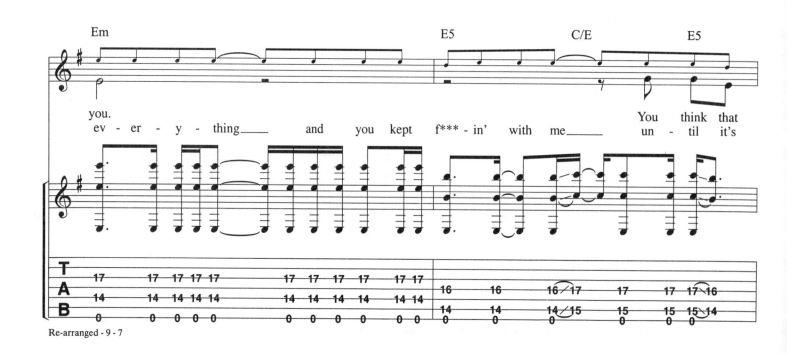

Re-arranged - 9 - 7

Re-arranged - 9 - 8

SMOOTH

Music and Lyrics by
ITAAL SHUR and ROB THOMAS

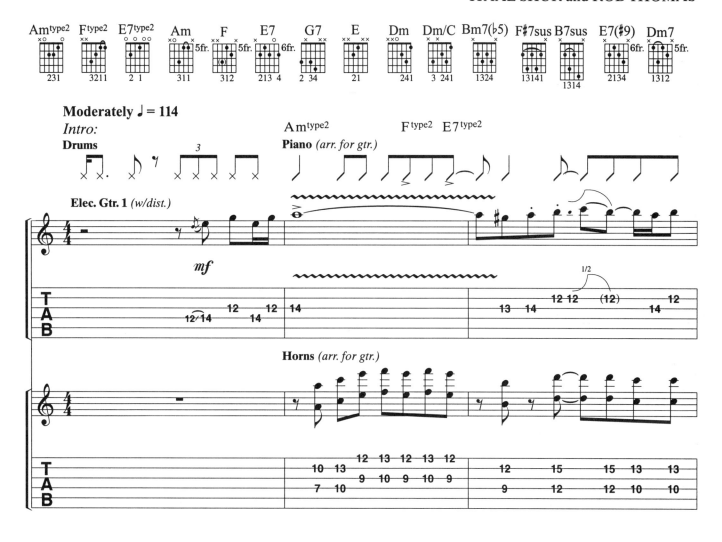

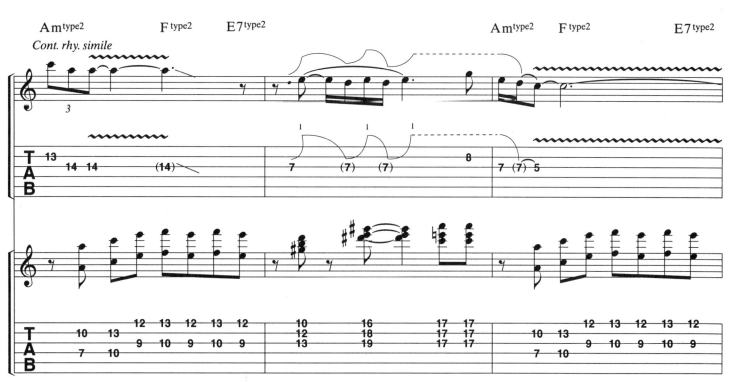

256

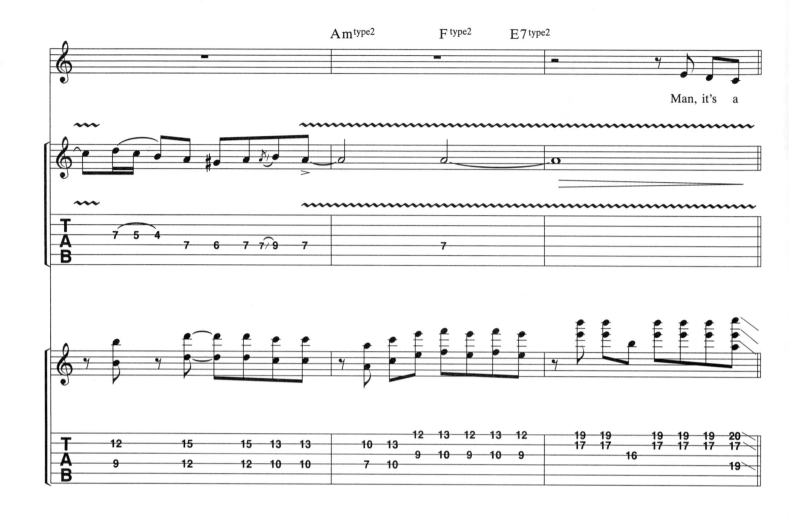

Man, it's a

Verse 1:

hot one, like sev - en inch - es from the mid - day sun.

Piano Rhy. Fig. 1

Smooth - 15 - 2

Well, I hear your whis-per and the words melt ev-'ry - one._____ But you stay___ so_

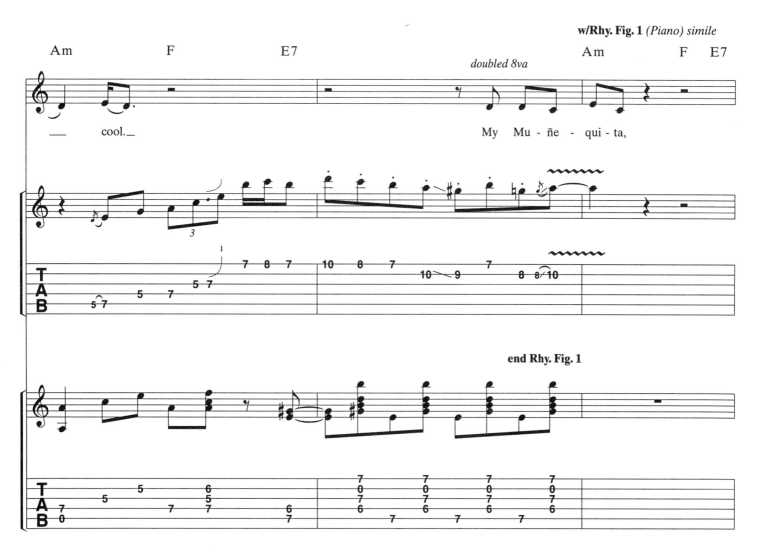

_ cool._ My Mu - ñe - qui - ta,

258

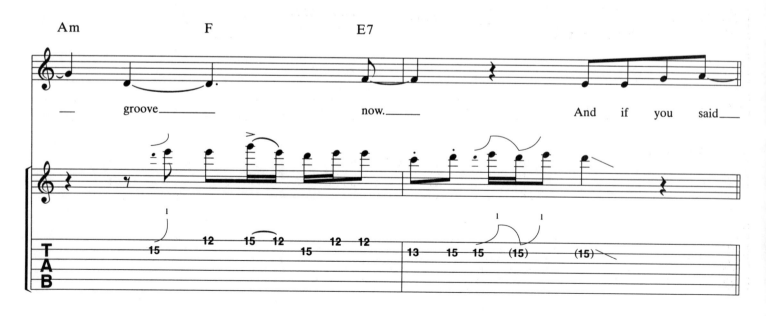

Smooth - 15 - 4

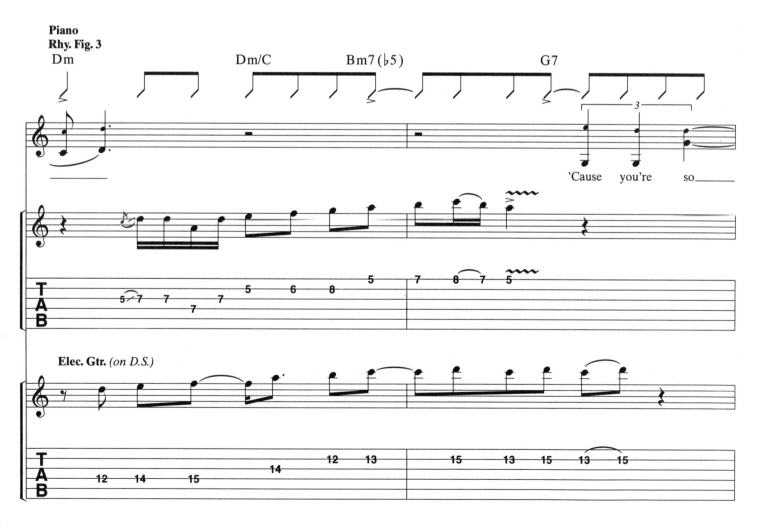

260

Smooth - 15 - 6

get from you.__ You got the kind of lov - ing that can be so smooth,_ yeah.

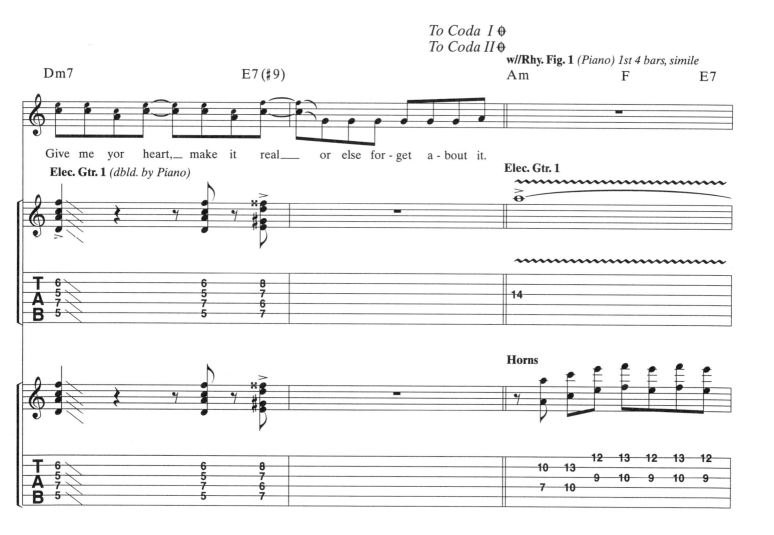

To Coda I
To Coda II

w//Rhy. Fig. 1 *(Piano) 1st 4 bars, simile*

Dm7   E7 (♯9)   Am   F   E7

Give me yor heart,_ make it real__ or else for - get a - bout it.

Elec. Gtr. 1 *(dbld. by Piano)*

Elec. Gtr. 1

Horns

Verse 2:
w/Rhy. Fig. 1 *(Piano) 2 times, simile*

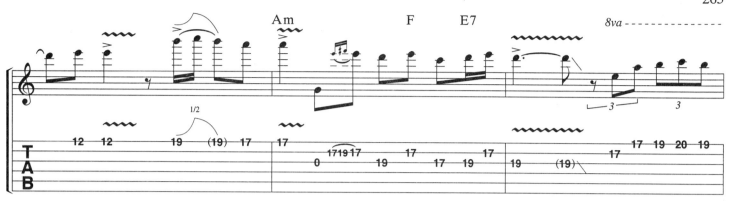

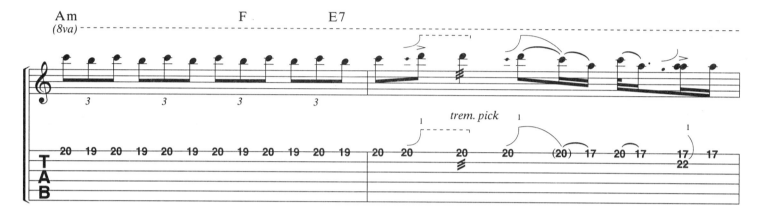

w/Rhy. Fig. 3 *(Piano) simile*

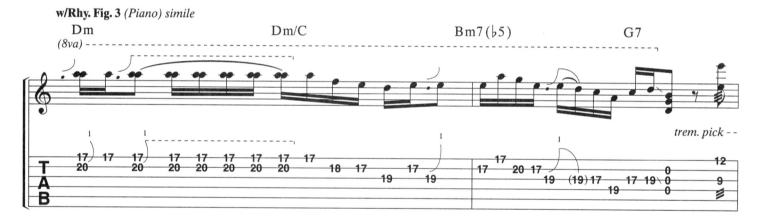

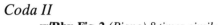

Coda II

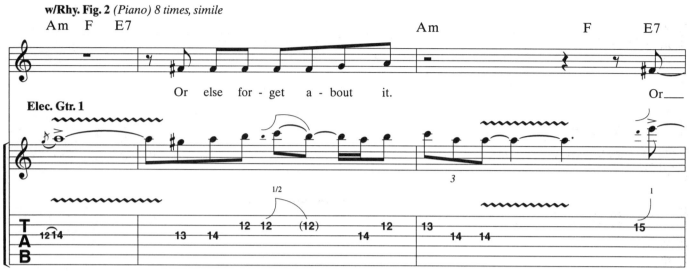

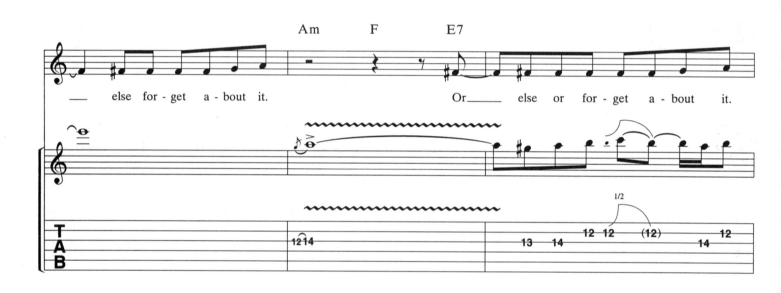

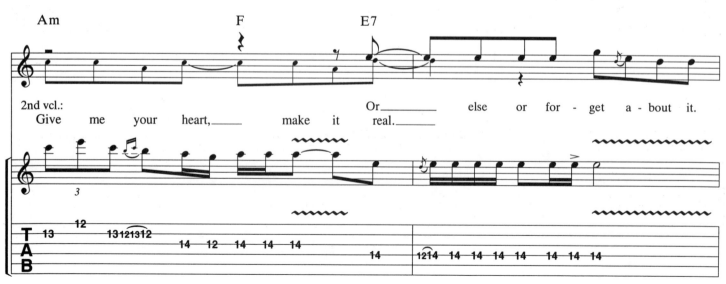

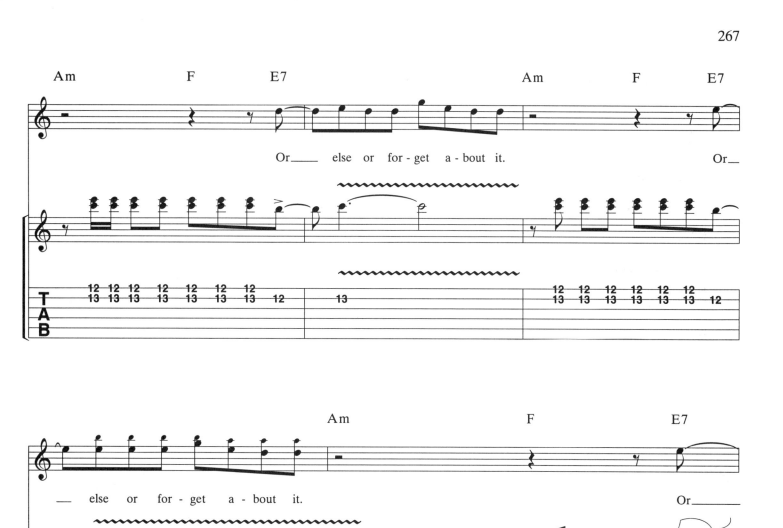

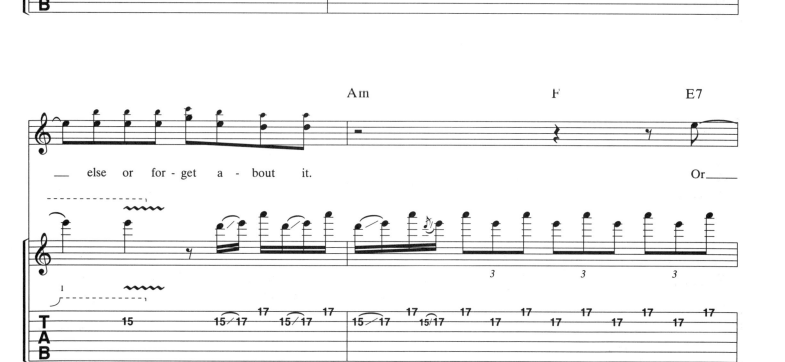

Smooth - 15 - 13

268

Outro:
wRhy. Fig. 2 *(Piano) 8 times, simile*

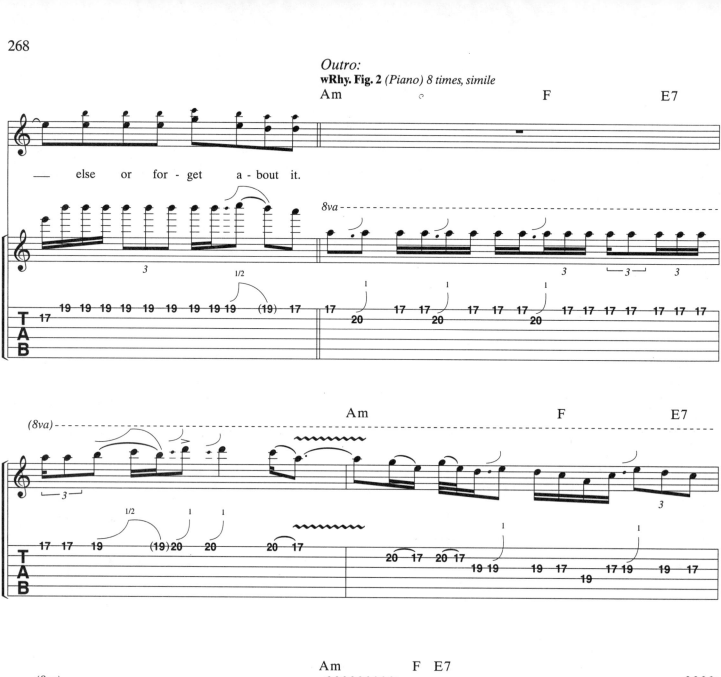

— else or for - get a - bout it.

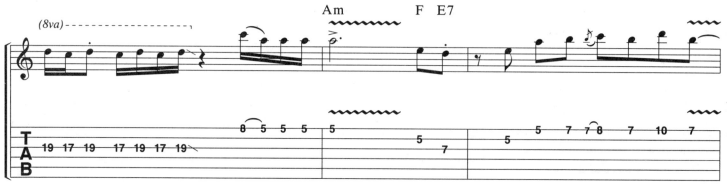

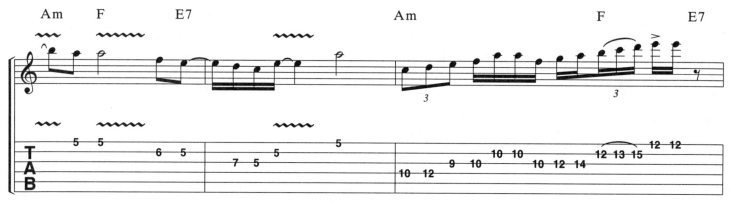

Smooth - 15 - 14

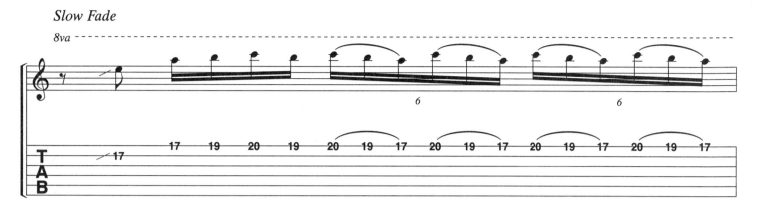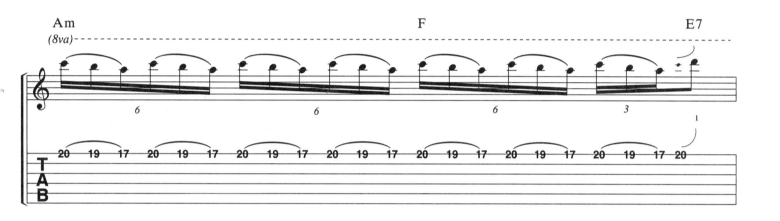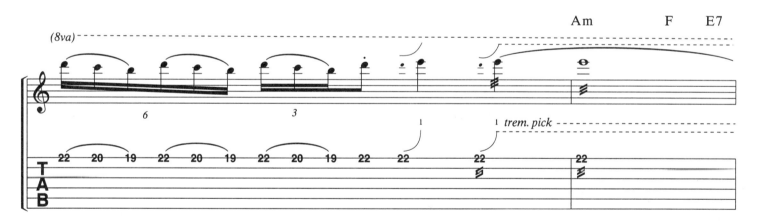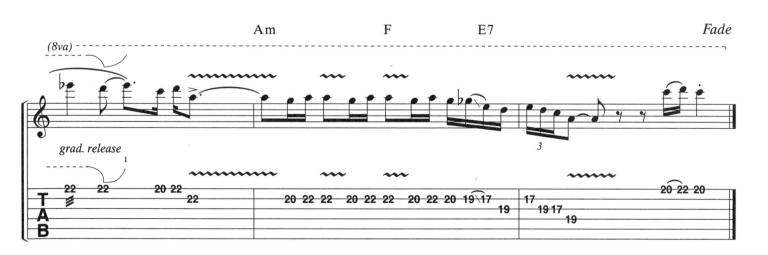

Smooth - 15 - 15

REVOLUTION IS MY NAME

Tune down 1 whole step:

⑥= D   ③= F
⑤= G   ②= A
④= C   ①= D

Words and Music by VINCENT ABBOTT, DARRELL ABBOTT,
PHILLIP ANSELMO and REX BROWN

Moderately / Tempo I ♩ = 96 (Half-time feel)

Intro:

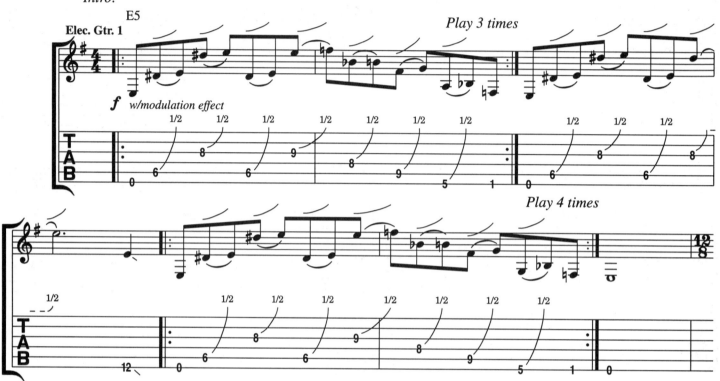

Faster
Tempo II ♩. = 138

Elec. Gtr. 1 tacet

E5

Riff A

*Elec. Gtrs. 2 & 3 play unison.

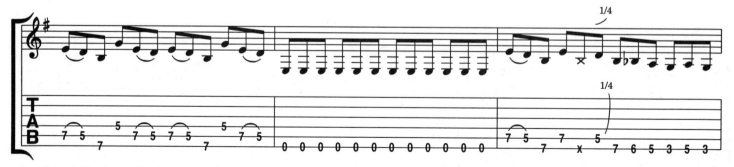

Revolution Is My Name – 10 – 1

Interlude 1:

Tempo I ♩ = 96

Elec. Gtr. 3 *(right)*

Riff B

Elec. Gtr. 2 *(left)*

Riff B1

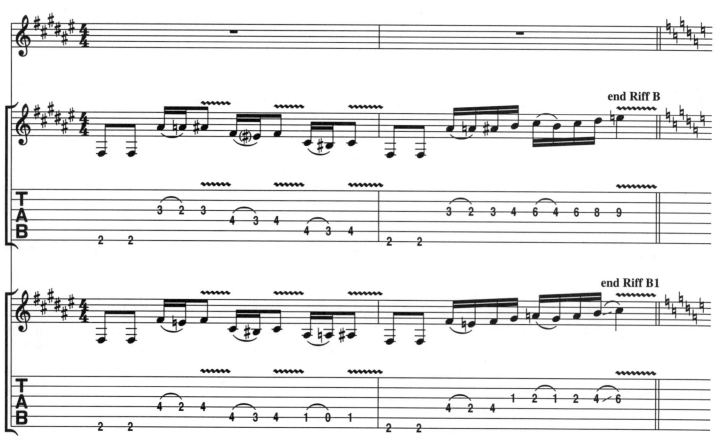

end Riff B

end Riff B1

276

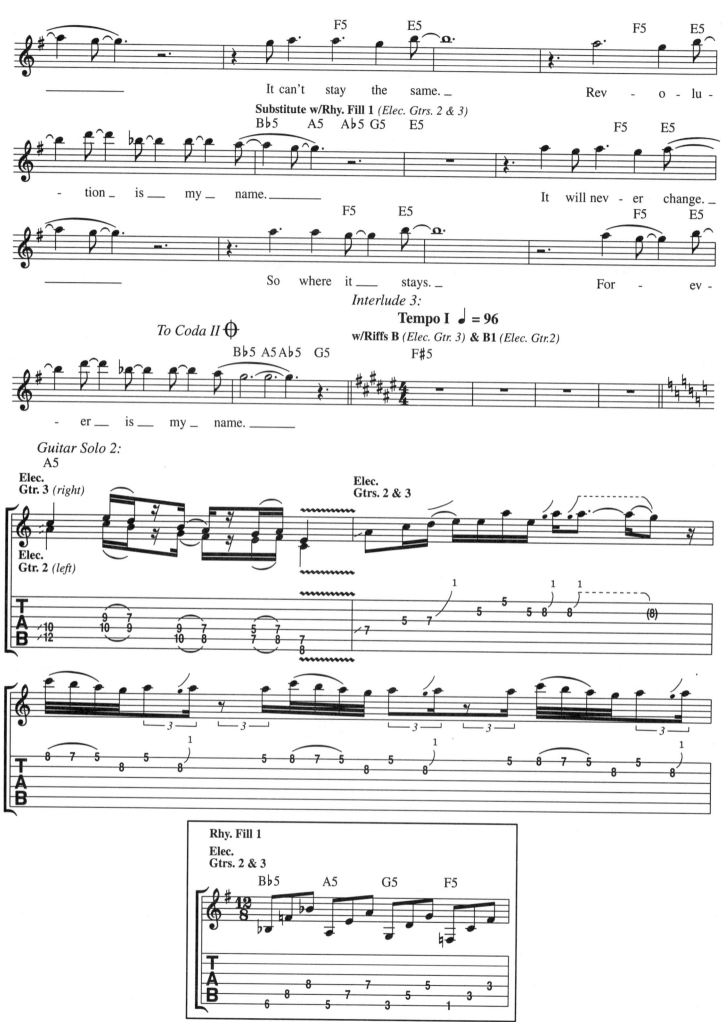

Revolution Is My Name – 10 – 7

Revolution Is My Name – 10 – 8

278

Bridge:

Midtro:
Tempo II ♩. = 138

Rev - o - lu - tion.

tion.

f w/slight P.M. throughout

D.S. 𝄌𝄌 al Coda II

Coda II

Revolution Is My Name – 10 – 10

RUN TO THE WATER

Words and Music by
Edward Kowalczyk and Patrick Dahlheimer

All gtrs. tune down 1/2 step:

⑥ = E♭   ③ = G♭
⑤ = A♭   ② = B♭
④ = D♭   ① = E♭

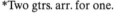

Moderately ♩ = 86

Intro:

*Two gtrs. arr. for one.

maker of children who weep for love,__ maker of__ this birth,__

__ 'til your deep-est se-crets are known to me, I will not be moved.__ I will not be moved.

Pre-chorus 1:

Don't__ try to find the an - swer,__ when there ain't no__ ques - tion here.

Elec. Gtr. 1
Rhy. Fig. 2
end Rhy. Fig. 2

w/Rhy. Fig. 1 *(Elec. Gtr. 1)*

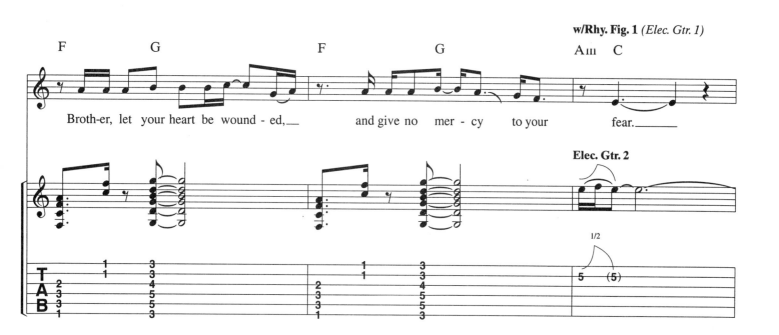

Broth-er, let your heart be wound - ed,__ and give no mer - cy to your fear._____

Elec. Gtr. 2

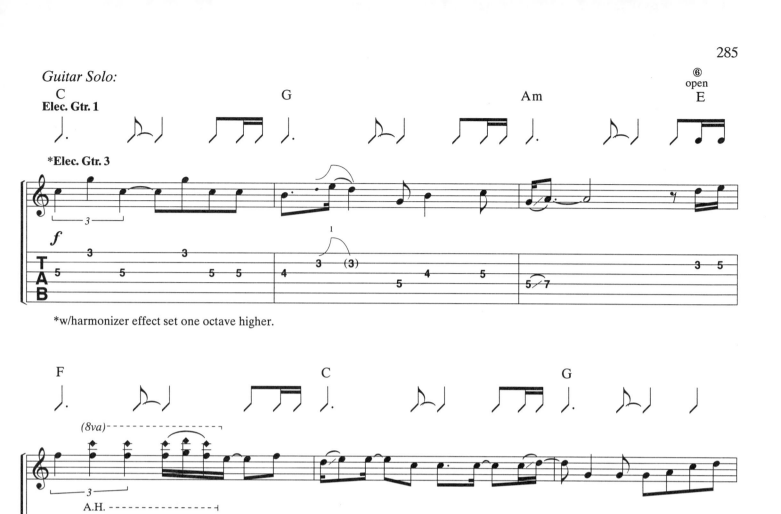

*w/harmonizer effect set one octave higher.

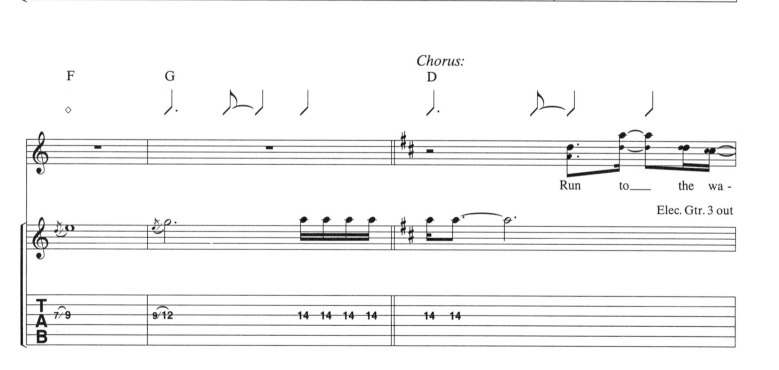

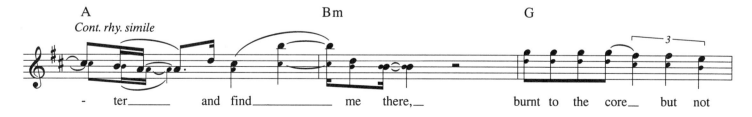

Run to___ the wa-

Elec. Gtr. 3 out

-ter___ and find___ me there,___ burnt to the core_ but not

Run to the Water - 8 - 6

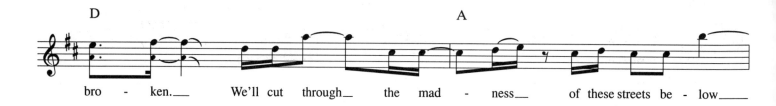

bro - ken.___ We'll cut through___ the mad - ness___ of these streets be - low___

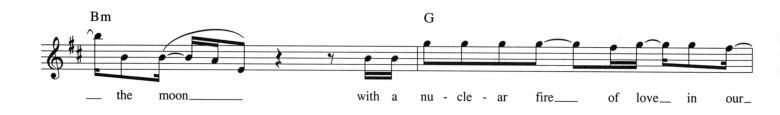

___ the moon_____ with a nu - cle - ar fire___ of love___ in our___

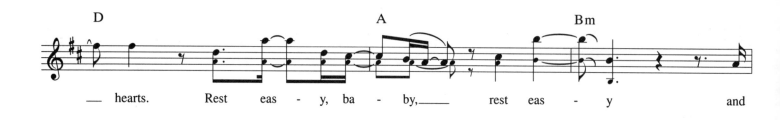

___ hearts. Rest eas - y, ba - by,___ rest eas - y and

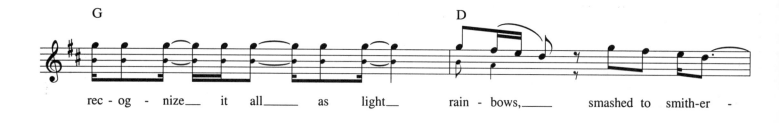

rec - og - nize___ it all___ as light___ rain - bows,___ smashed to smith-er -

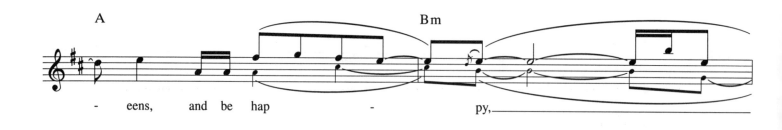

- eens, and be hap - py,_____

___ yeah._____ Run to___ the wa - ter_____ and find_____

286

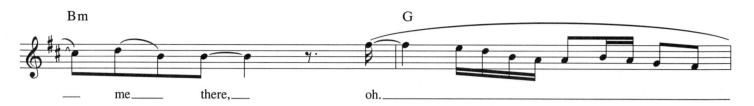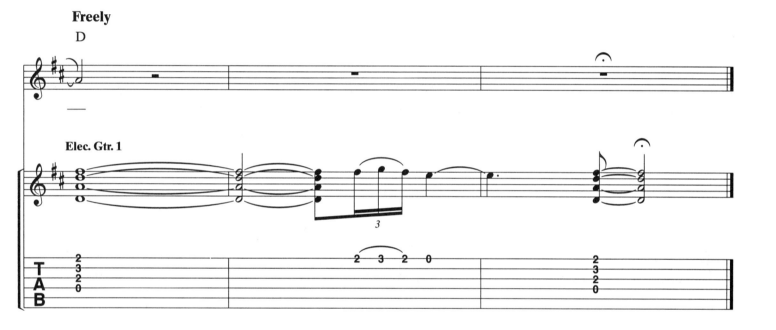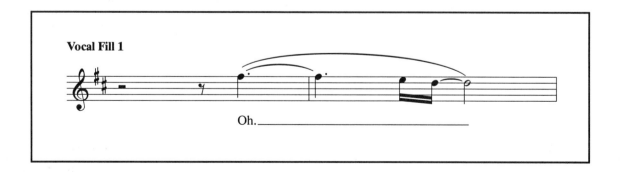

Run to the Water - 8 - 8

SIMPLE KIND OF LIFE

Words and Music by
GWEN STEFANI

Simple Kind of Life - 12 - 1

Simple Kind of Life - 12 - 2

*Bass gtr. plays G.

Simple Kind of Life - 12 - 4

292

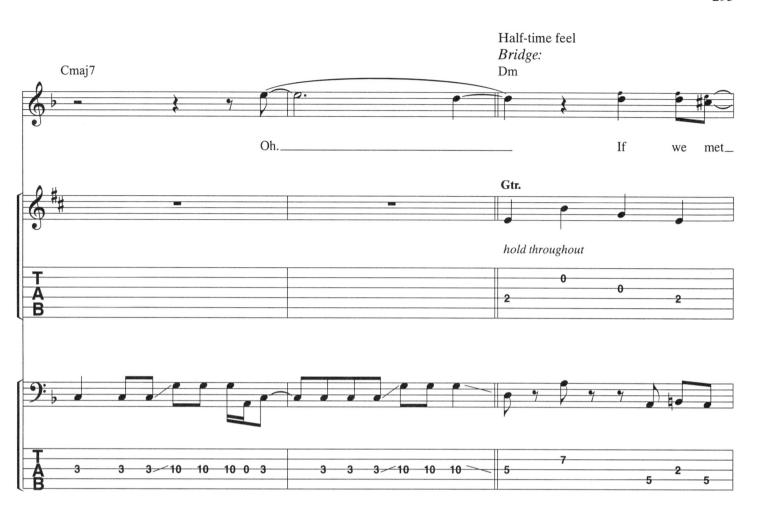

294

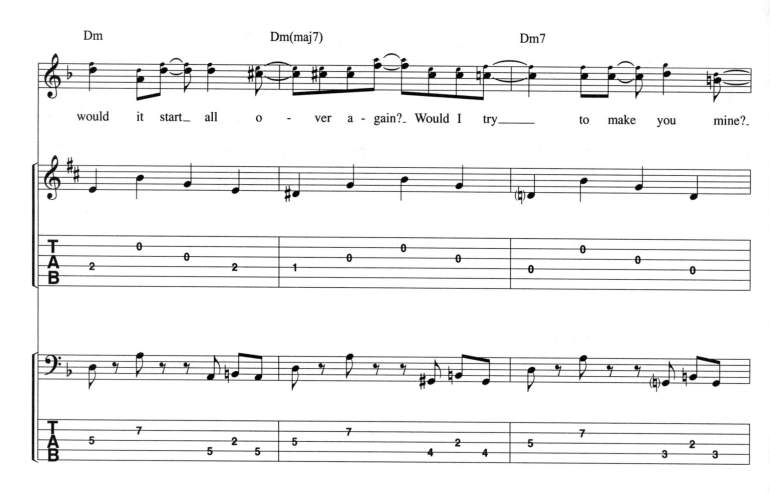

would it start_ all o - ver a - gain?_ Would I try_____ to make you mine?_

Verse 3:

I al - ways thought_ I'd be a mom._

Simple Kind of Life - 12 - 7

296

Simple Kind of Life - 12 - 9

Simple Kind of Life - 12 - 10

298

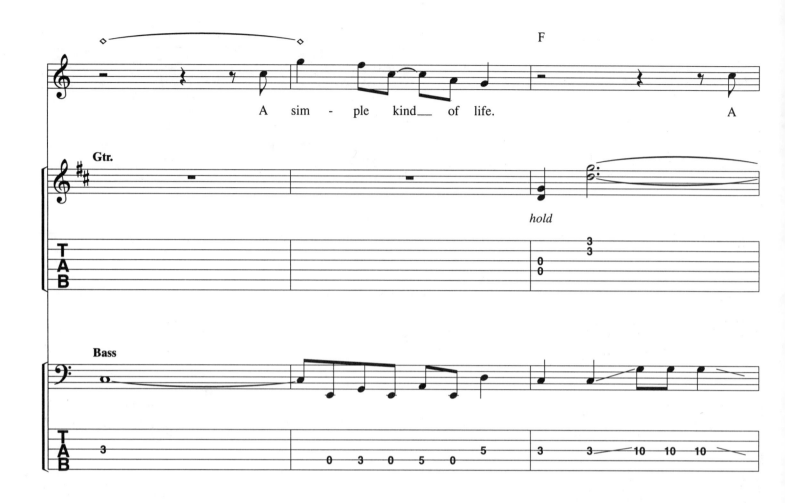

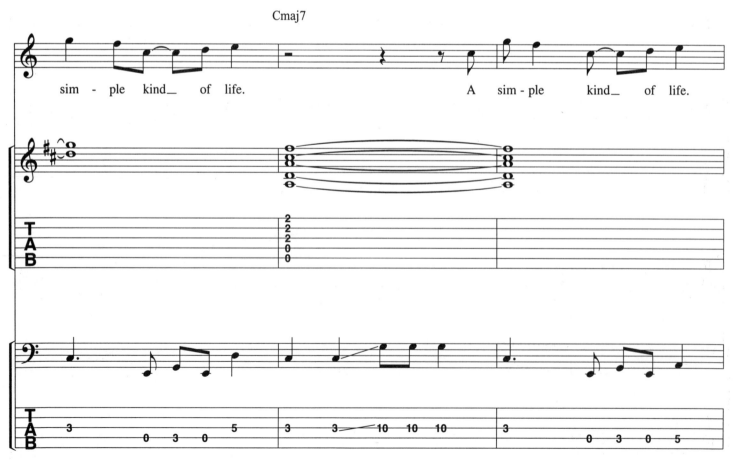

Simple Kind of Life - 12 - 11

SOMEBODY SOMEONE

Somebody Someone – 5 – 1

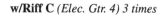

w/Riff C (Elec. Gtr. 4) 3 times

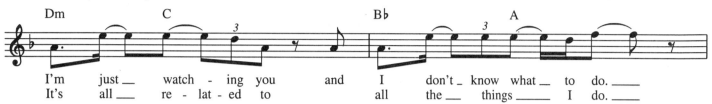

I'm just __ watch - ing you and I don't _ know what _ to do. __
It's all __ re - lat - ed to all the __ things ____ I do. __

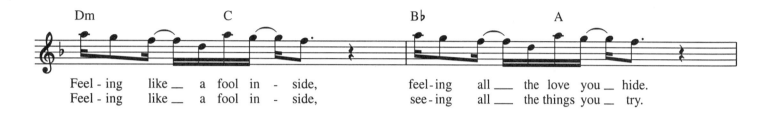

Feel - ing like __ a fool in - side, feel-ing all __ the love you _ hide.
Feel - ing like __ a fool in - side, see-ing all __ the things you _ try.

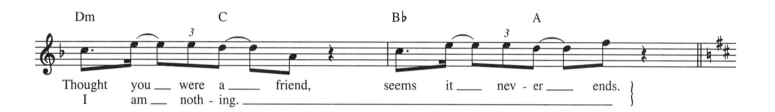

Thought you _ were a ____ friend, seems it __ nev - er __ ends.
I am __ noth - ing. _____

Pre-chorus:
w/Riff B (Elec. Gtrs. 2 & 3) 2 times

I need _____ some - bod - y, some - one.

Chorus:

Can some - bod-y help me! _____ All I need is to be. _

Somebody Someone – 5 – 2

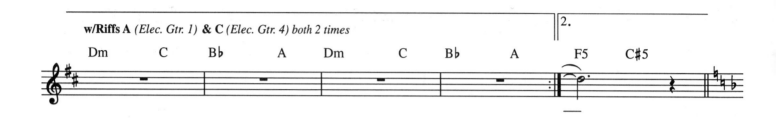

Somebody Someone – 5 – 4

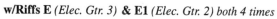

w/Riffs E *(Elec. Gtr. 3)* **& E1** *(Elec. Gtr. 2) both 4 times*

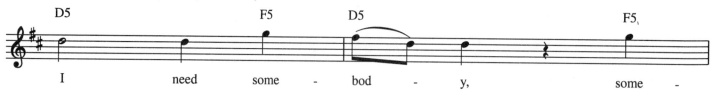

I need some - bod - y, some -

bod - y, some - one. _____ I need some -

bod - y, some - bod - y, some - one. _____

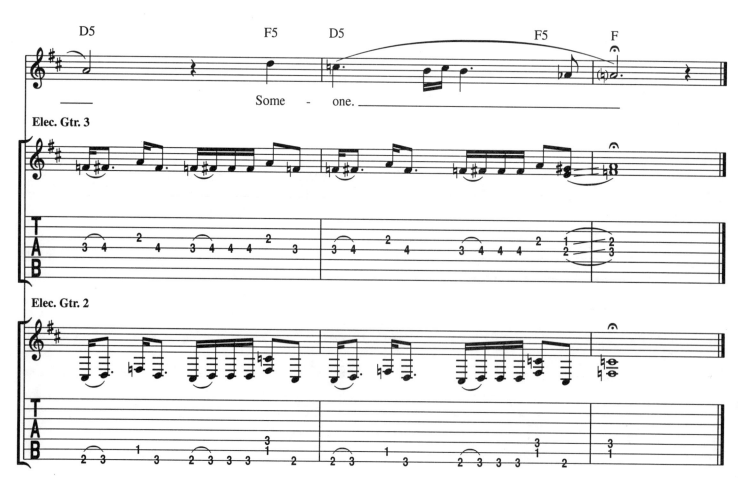

____ Some - one. _____

Elec. Gtr. 3

Elec. Gtr. 2

Someday

Words and Music by MARK McGRATH, STAN FRAZIER,
RODNEY SHEPPARD, MATTHEW MURPHY KARGES,
CRAIG BULLOCK, JOSEPH "MCG" NICHOL and DAVID KAHNE

306

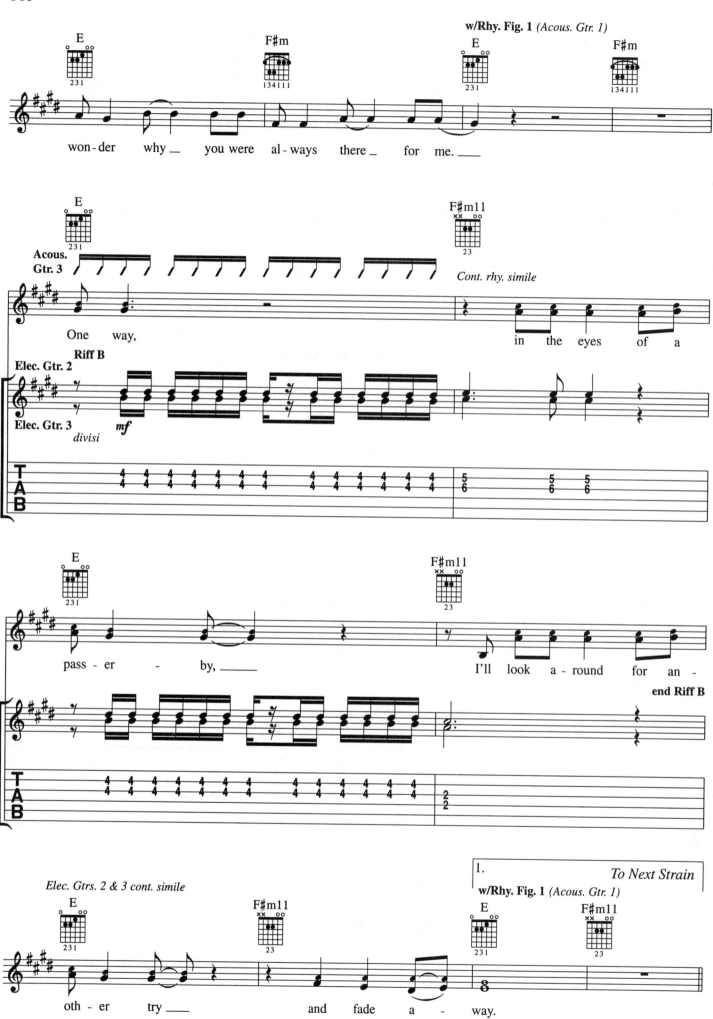

Someday – 7 – 2

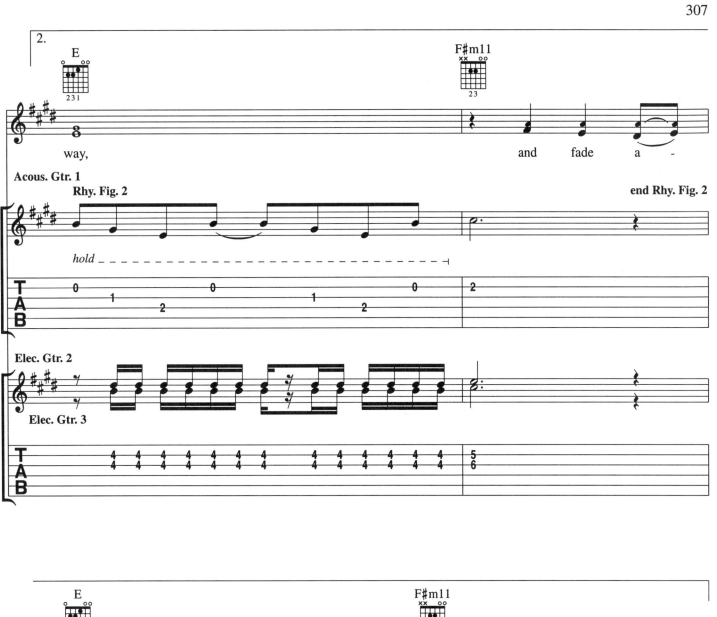

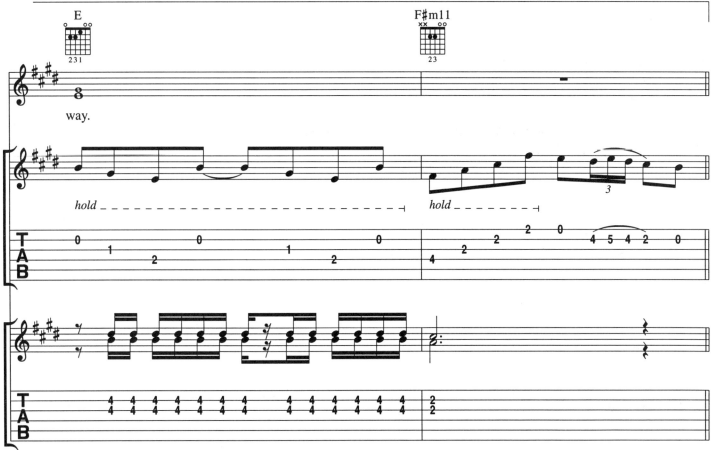

308

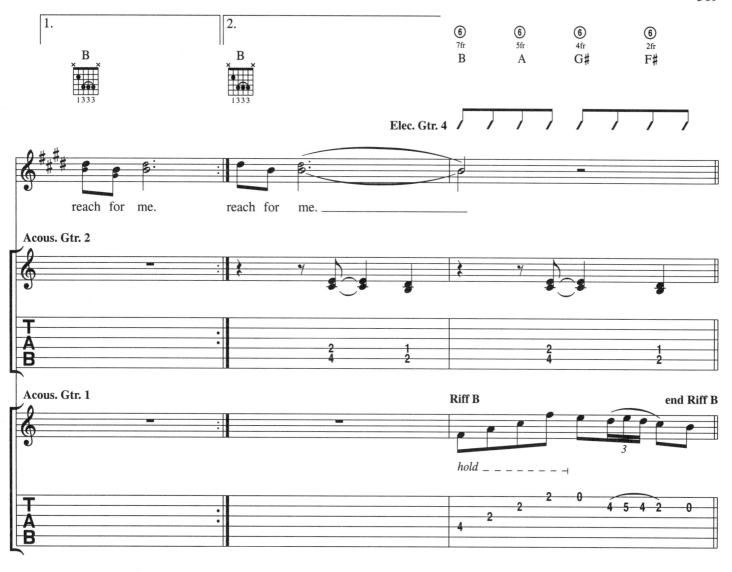

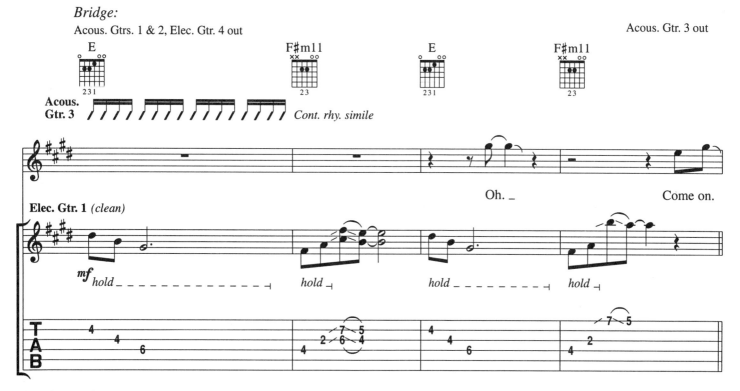

Someday – 7 – 5

SOUR GIRL

Words and Music by
DEAN DELEO, ROBERT DELEO,
ERIC KRETZ and SCOTT WEILAND

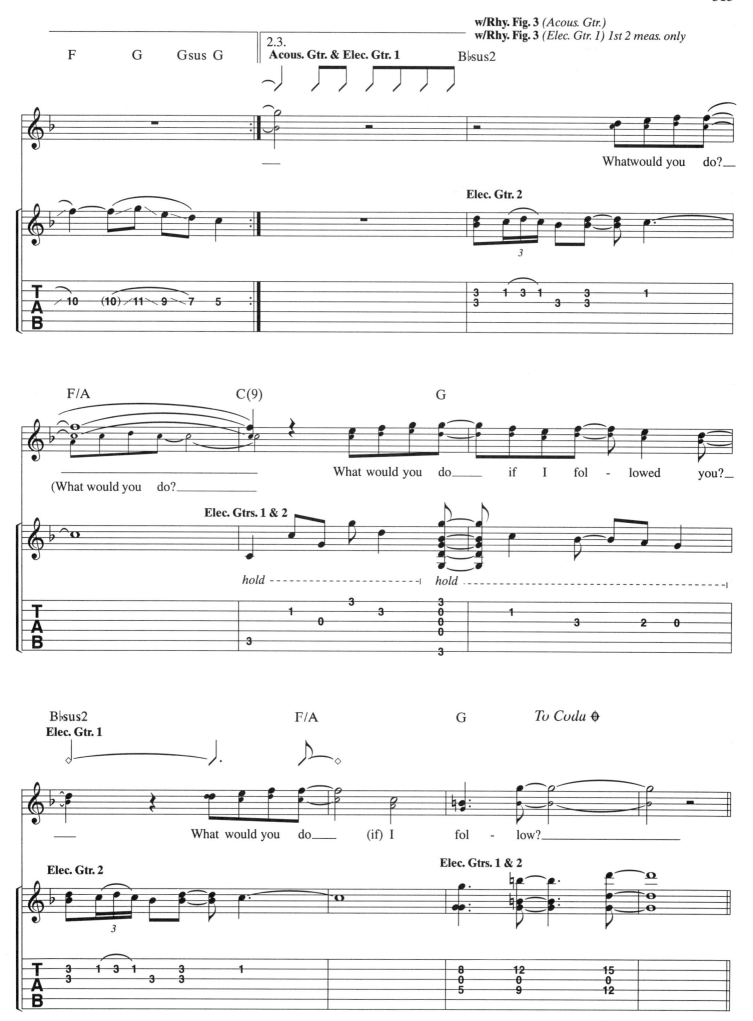

316

Sour Girl - 6 - 5

Outro:
w/Rhy. Fig. 2 *(Acous. Gtr.) till fade*

Verse 2:
Don't turn away; what are you looking at?
He was so happy on the day that he met her.
Say, what are you looking at?
I was a superman, but looks are deceiving.
The rollercoaster ride's a lonely one,
I'd pay a ransom note to stop it from steaming.
Hey! What are you looking at?
She was a teenage girl when she met me.
(To Chorus:)

STUPIFY

Drop D tuning:
Tune down 1/2 step:
⑥=Db ③=Gb
⑤=Ab ②=Bb
④=Db ①=Eb

Words and Music by
**MIKE WENGREN, DAN DONEGAN,
DAVE DRAIMAN and STEVE "FUZZ" KMAK**

Moderately ♩ = 98
Intro:

(Spoken:) Yeah,

bringing you another disturbing creation from the mind of one sick animal who can't tell the

Stupify - 7 - 1

320

*+ = closed wah (back position).
o = open wah (front position).

323

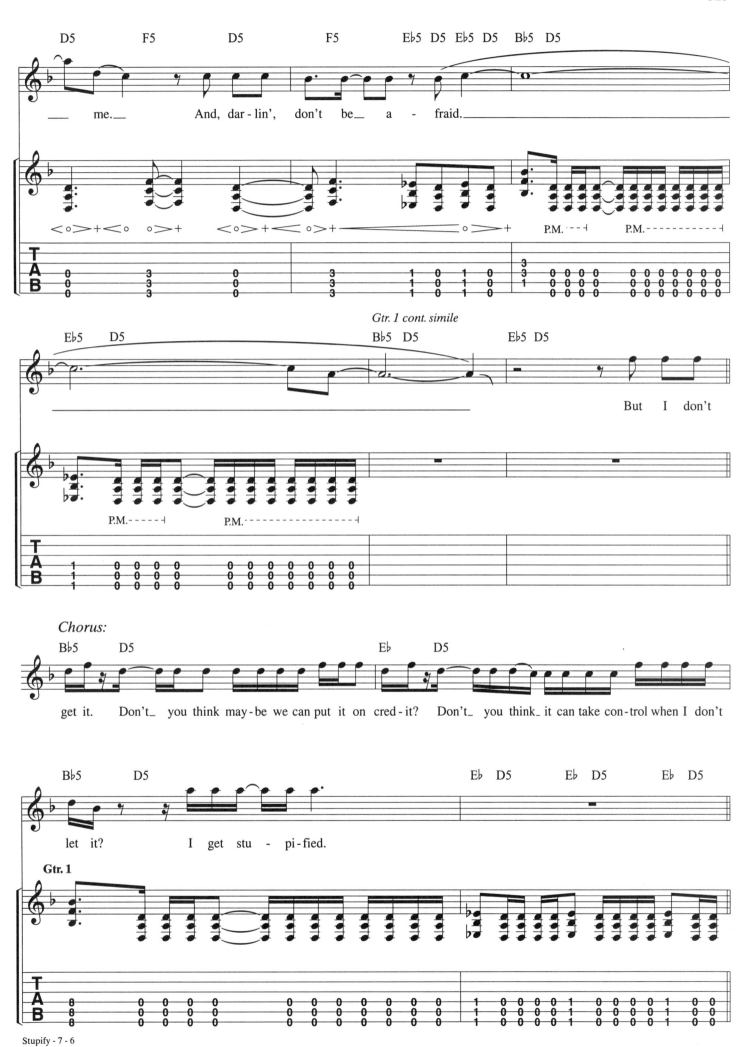

Stupify - 7 - 6

THEN THE MORNING COMES

Words and Music by
GREG CAMP

Tune down 1/2 step:
⑥= E♭ ③= G♭
⑤= A♭ ②= B♭
④= D♭ ①= E♭

Moderately ♩ = 118

Intro:

Gtr. 1

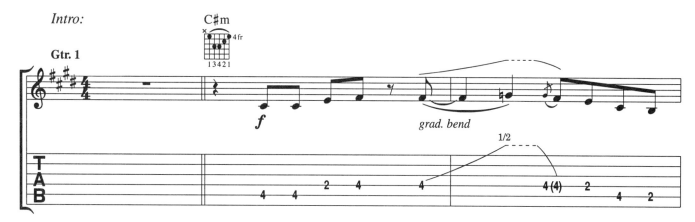

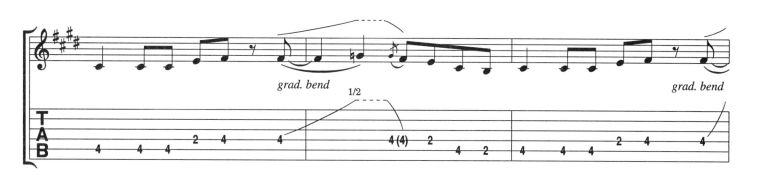

Then the Morning Comes – 5 – 1

326

Then the Morning Comes – 5 – 2

Then the Morning Comes – 5 – 3

328

Then the Morning Comes – 5 – 4

329

Then the Morning Comes – 5 – 5

THE BAD TOUCH

Words and Music by
JIMMY FRANKS

Composite arrangement.

The Bad Touch - 4 - 1

332

The Bad Touch - 4 - 3

Chorus:

You and me ba - by ain't noth - in' but mam - mals so let's do it like they do on the Dis -

cov - er - y Chan - nel *Do it a - gain now* You and me ba - by ain't noth - in' but mam - mals so let's

do it like they do on the Dis - cov - er - y Chan - nel *Do it now* cov - er - y Chan - nel *Get-tin' horn - y now.*

Outro:

w/Rhy. Fig. 1 *(Bass) simile*   *Play 6 times and fade*

Horns

Verse 2:
Love the kind you clean up with a mop and bucket
Like the lost catacombs of Egypt only God knows where we stuck it
Hieroglyphics? Let me be Pacific wanna be down in your South Seas
But I got this notion that the motion of your ocean means "Small Craft Advisory"
So if I capsize on your thighs high tide B-5 you sunk my battleship
Please turn me on I'm Mister Coffee with an automatic drip
So show me yours I'll show you mine "Tool Time" you'll Lovett just like Lyle
And then we'll do it doggy style so we can both watch "X-Files"
(To Chorus:)

The Bad Touch - 4 - 4

THE DOLPHIN'S CRY

Words and Music by
Edward Kowalczyk

The way you're bathed in light___ re - minds me of that night___

God laid me down in - to your rose_____ gar - den of trust.___

___ And I was swept a - way___ with noth - in' left to say.___

The Dolphin's Cry - 10 - 1

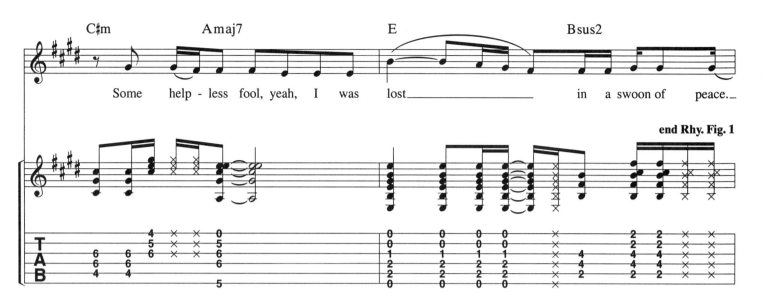

Some help - less fool, yeah, I was lost_____ in a swoon of peace._

end Rhy. Fig. 1

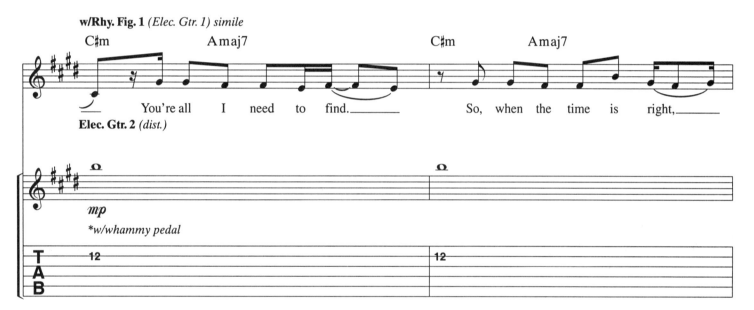

w/Rhy. Fig. 1 *(Elec. Gtr. 1) simile*

You're all I need to find._____ So, when the time is right,_____

Elec. Gtr. 2 *(dist.)*

mp

*w/whammy pedal

*Set to produce pitches one octave above fretted notes.

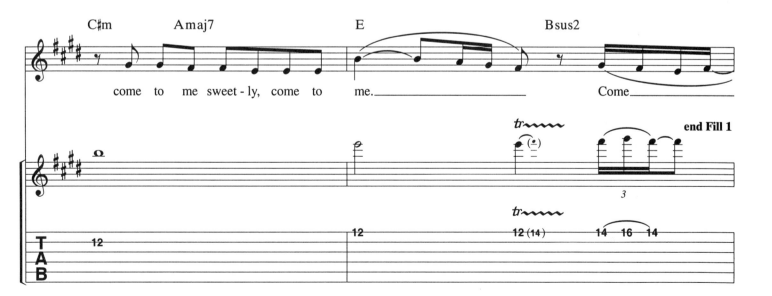

come to me sweet - ly, come to me._____ Come_____

end Fill 1

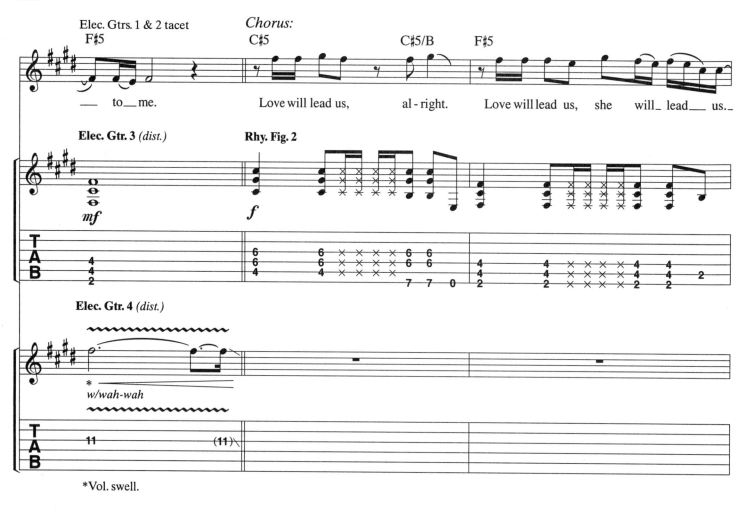

*Vol. swell.

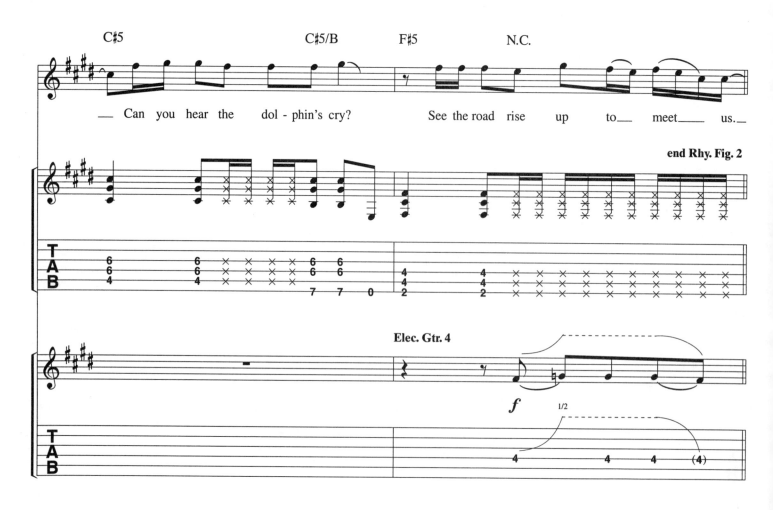

The Dolphin's Cry - 10 - 4

338

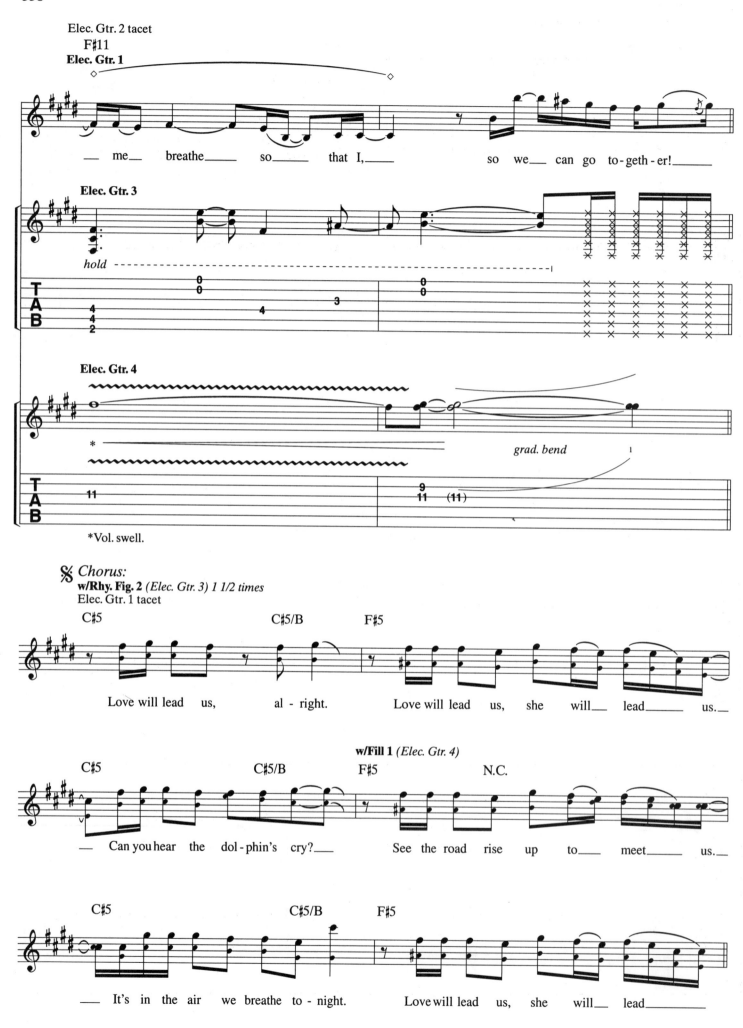

The Dolphin's Cry - 10 - 5

340

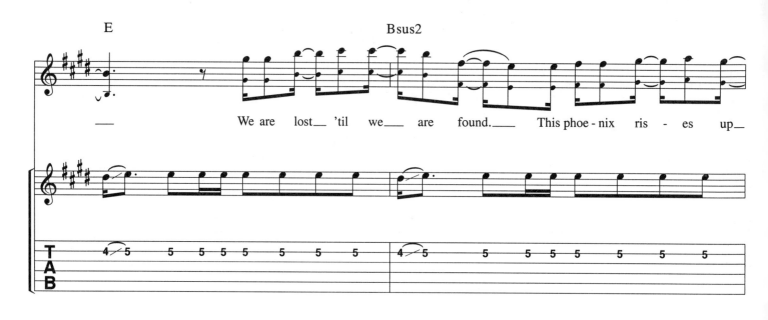

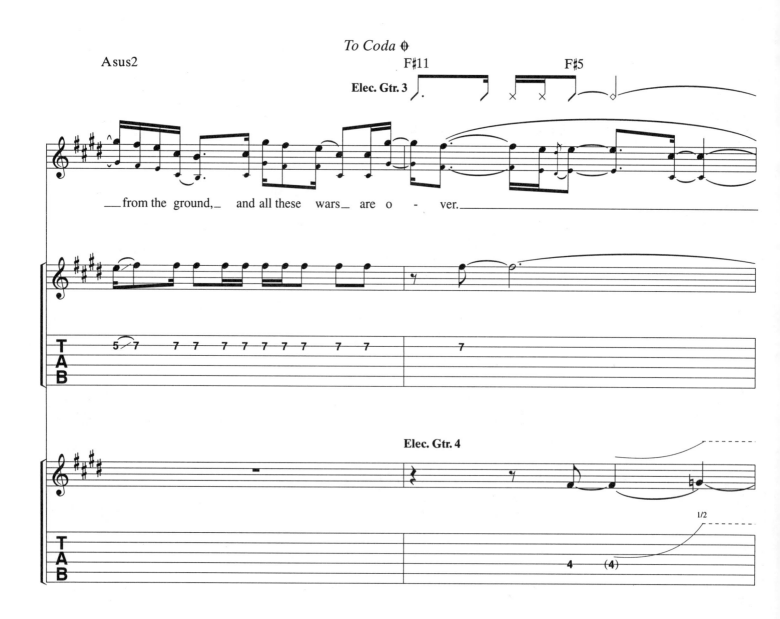

The Dolphin's Cry - 10 - 7

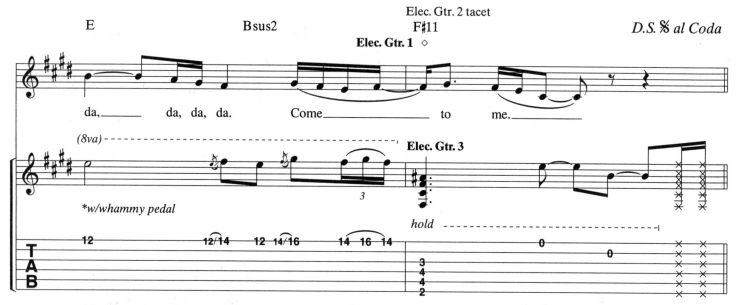

*Set to produce pitches one octave above fretted notes.

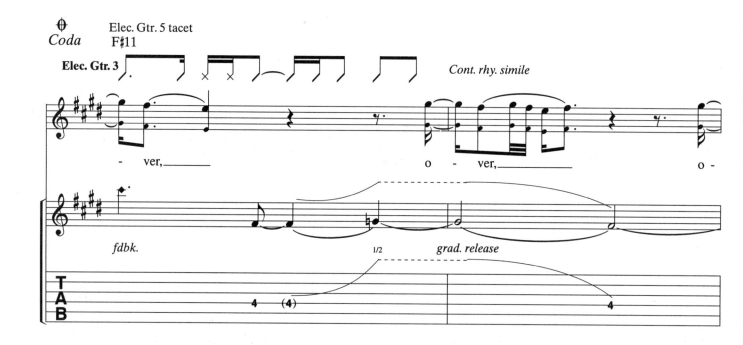

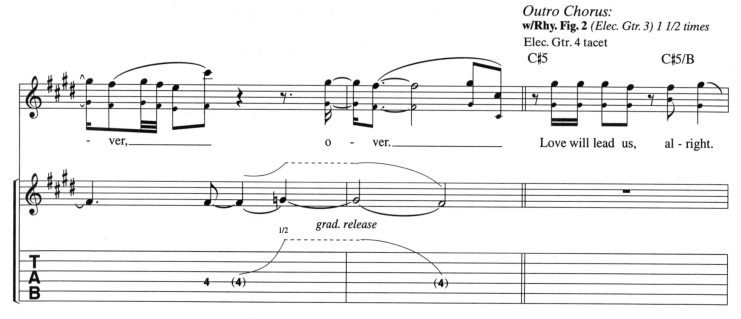

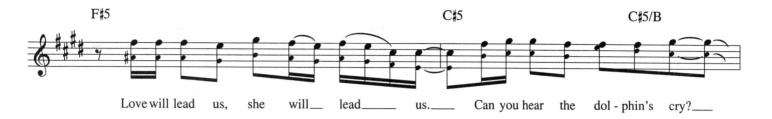

Love will lead us, she will lead us. Can you hear the dol-phin's cry?

See the road rise up to meet us. It's in the air we breathe to-night.

Begin fade
w/Rhy. Fig. 2 *(Elec. Gtr. 3) 1 1/4 times*

Love will lead us, she will lead us. Whoa,_ yeah,_
(Love will lead us, al - right.

al - right._ Al - right.
Do it o - ver, she will lead us. Love will lead us, al - right.

Fade

Al - right.
If you sur - ren - der, love will save us. Love will lead us, al - right.)

The Dolphin's Cry - 10 - 10

THEY STOOD UP FOR LOVE

Words and Music by
Edward Kowalczyk, Chad Taylor and Patrick Dahlheimer

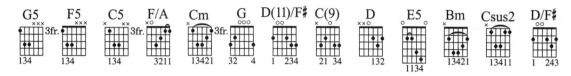

All gtrs. tune down 1/2 step:

⑥ = E♭   ③ = G♭
⑤ = A♭   ② = B♭
④ = D♭   ① = E♭

Moderately slow ♩ = 94

Intro:

Cont. rhy. simile throughout
(unless otherwise indicated)

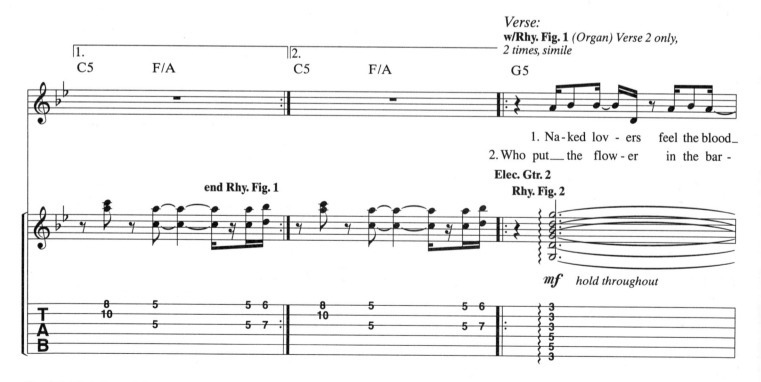

1. Na-ked lov-ers   feel the blood
2. Who put   the flow-er   in the bar-

mf hold throughout

They Stood Up for Love - 8 - 1

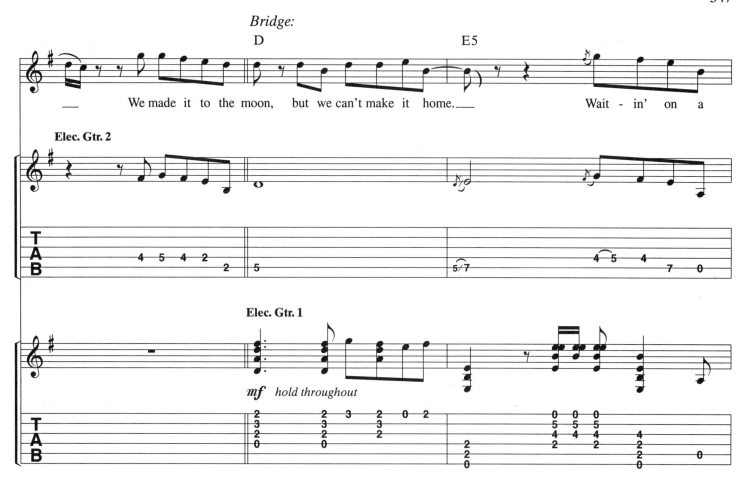

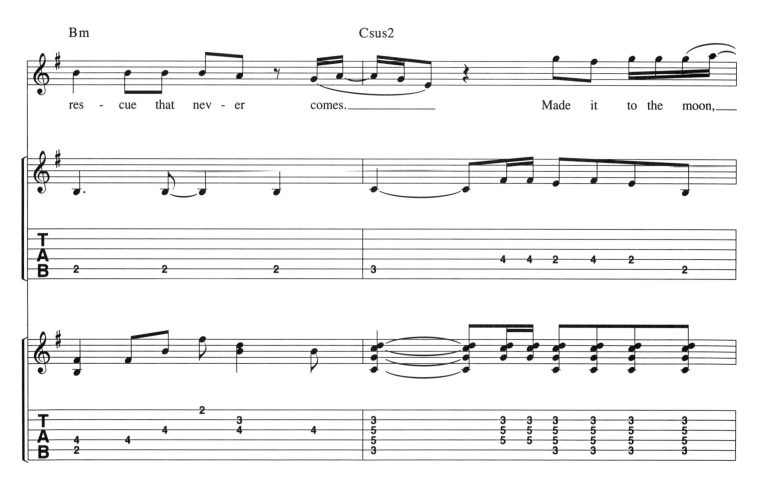

348

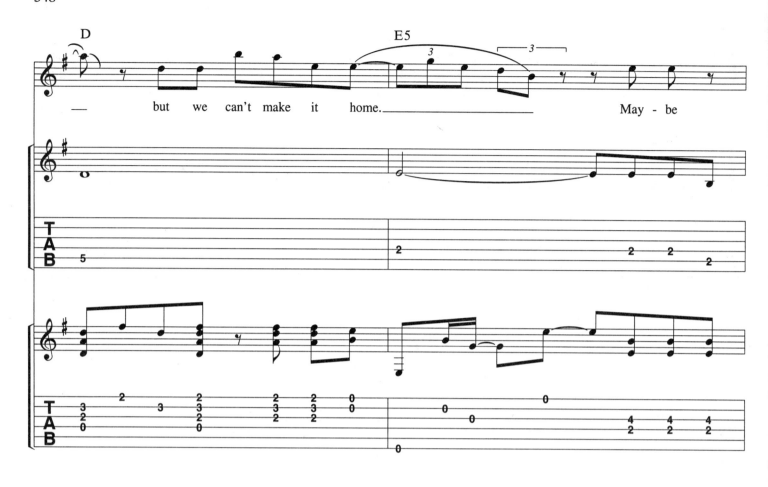

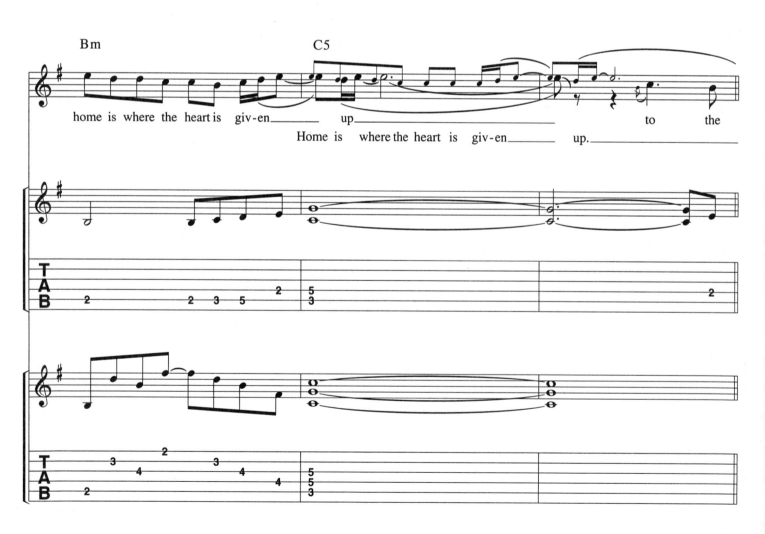

They Stood Up for Love - 8 - 5

one, to the one.

Elec. Gtr. 2

We spend all of our lives going out of our minds. Look-in' back to our birth,

Elec. Gtr. 2

for - ward to our de - mise.
Ah.
We spend all of our____ lives____

G

D(11)/F♯   C(9)

go - ing out of our minds.____   They live,   they,____

G
*Elec. Gtr. 1

____ they stood up for love,____   stood up for love,____

Synth. (arr. for gtr.)   Synth. Riff 1

*2 gtrs. arr. for 1 to end.

stood up for love,_____ yeah,_____ yeah._____

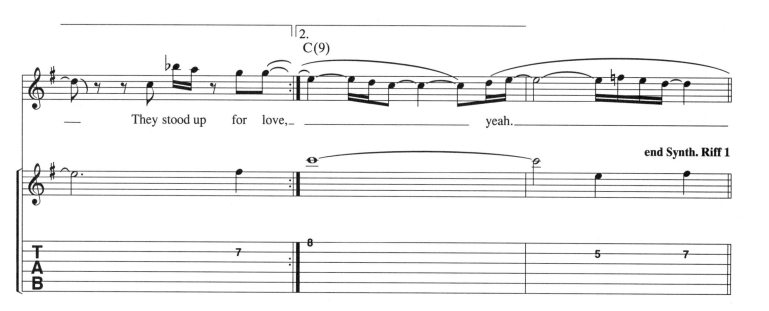

They stood up for love,_ _____ yeah._____

end Synth. Riff 1

Outro:
w/Bkgd. Vcl. Fig. 1 & Riff 1 *(Synth.) both simile*

Repeat and fade

We spend all of our lives___ go-ing out of our minds._____

Mas-ters in ev-'ry time._

*Lead vcl. ad lib. on repeats.

They Stood Up for Love - 8 - 8

TREMBLE FOR MY BELOVED

Words and Music by
ED ROLAND

All gtrs. tune down 1/2 step:
⑥ = Eb ③ = Gb
⑤ = Ab ② = Bb
④ = Db ① = Eb

*Bkwds. gtr. arr. for standard gtr.

Tremble for My Beloved – 6 – 1

end Riff A

Bass & Drums

The hour _____ has __ be - gun. _

Verse:

D

* Gtr. 2   Cont. rhy. simile

Gtr. 3

Riff B   end Riff B

* Rock wah pedal with an eighth-note rhythm pattern.

Tremble for My Beloved – 6 – 2

354

Tremble for My Beloved – 6 – 4

356

Tremble for My Beloved – 6 – 5

Tremble for My Beloved – 6 – 6

VOODOO

Words and Music by
SULLY ERNA and ROB MERRILL

Voodoo - 4 - 1

no more rea - son to stay. Freez - ing feel -
why my thoughts aren't so clear. De - mons dream -

ing, breathe in, breathe in.
ing, breathe in, breathe in.

I'm com - ing

𝄋 Chorus

back a - gain.

I'm not the one who's so far a - way when I

Gtr. 1

Rhy. Fig. 2

P.M.

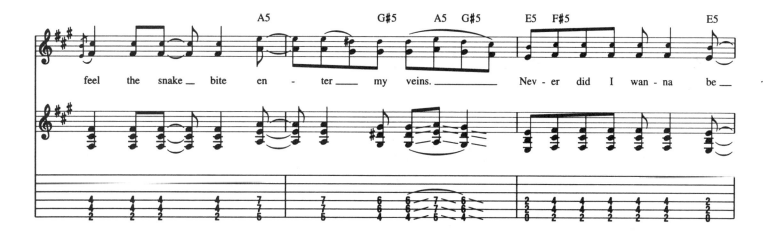

feel the snake bite en - ter my veins. Nev - er did I wan - na be

1.

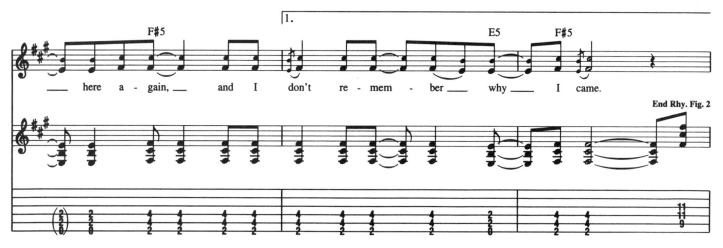

here a - gain, and I don't re - mem - ber why I came.

End Rhy. Fig. 2

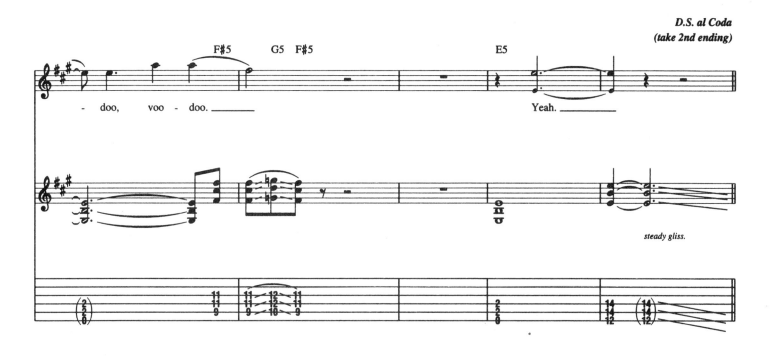

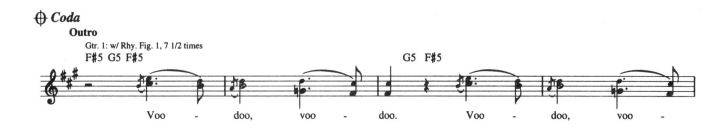

Voodoo - 4 - 4

WAS

Words and Music by
KENNY WAYNE SHEPHERD,
MARK SELBY and TIA SILLERS

Was – 13 – 1

366

Was – 13 – 5

*Composite arrangement.

Was – 13 – 6

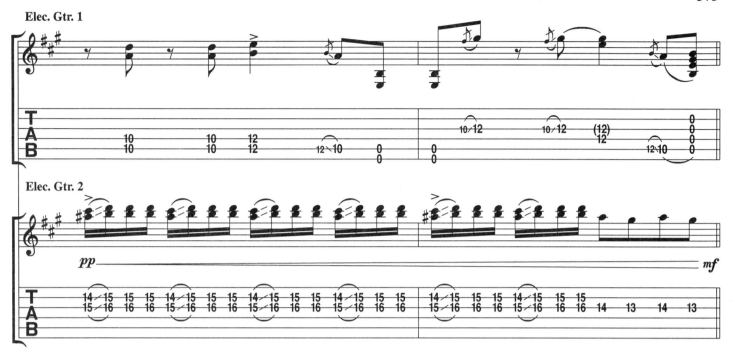

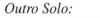

Outro Solo:
w/Rhy. Fig. 1 *(Dobro, dbld. by Elec. Gtr. 1) 11 measures only, simile*

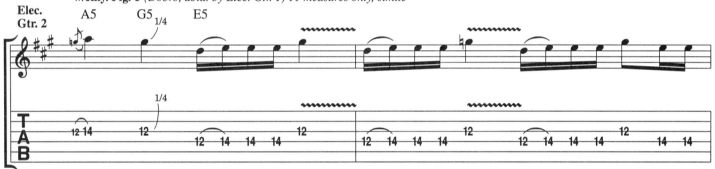

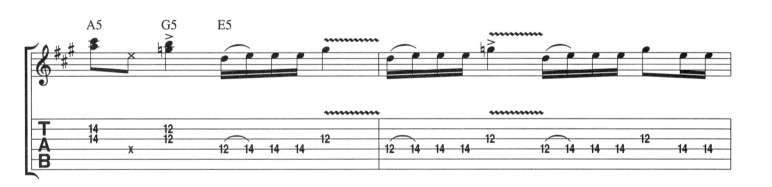

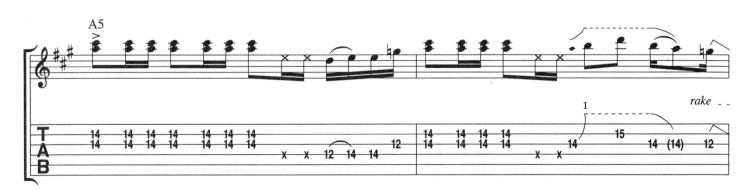

Was – 13 – 12

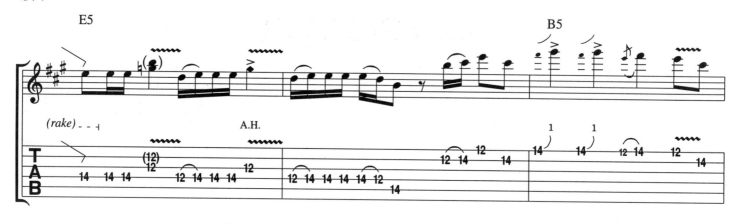

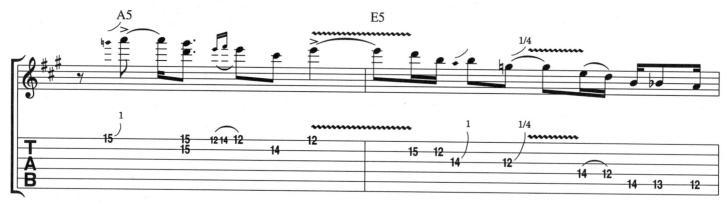

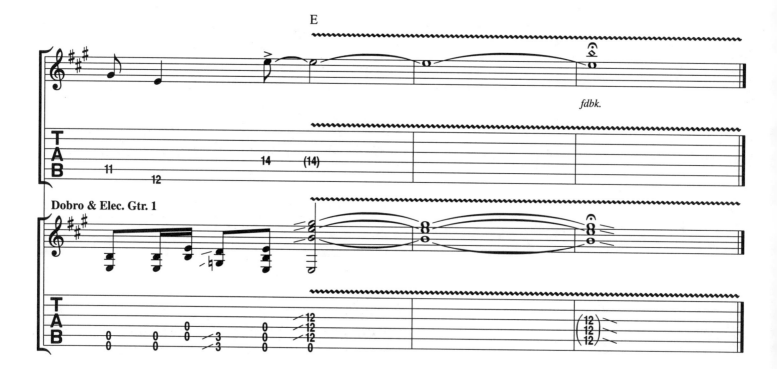

Verse 4:
She was a long way home,
Walking broken bone.
It was wrong or right,
How deep that knife could go.
It was a crazy thought;
A madman's walk it was.
It was a crazy thought;
A madman's walk it was.
She was the hangman's noose,
I was the fool, I was.
Oh, I was.
Yeah, baby, I was, oo . . .

WASTING TIME

**Words and Music by
ROBERT "KID ROCK" RITCHIE,
LINDSEY BUCKINGHAM
and MATTHEW SHAFER**

Wasting Time – 7 – 1

roll-in' a Fleet-wood, that's how I mack. _ I rock all the tracks, _ so the world knows _ I love
Pay-in' dues, drink - in' Boone's. Writ - in' tunes, and hop - in' to get

all the girls, _ smack all the ho's. _ Show love to those _ who come real with it.
one of these moth - er f*** - ing songs to hit. A lit - tle bit of love, that's all I need. A lit-tle

Life's a bitch _ but I deal with it. I'm in it to win it like Y - zer - man. _ Can
in - spi - ra - tion and a bag of weed. A seed to plant so my tree can grow. Ya know I

drink a-bout fif - teen Hein - e - kens. _ I'm not born a - gain, _ but if I was, _ I'd
left my girl 'cuz I don't need that. _ Hold up, wait a min-ute I'm a-bout to flow. Like a

Elec. Gtr. 1

mp

Elec. Gtr. 3 (clean-tone)

mf

*Play on 1st verse only.

Wasting Time – 7 – 2

Wasting Time – 7 – 3

378

380

Wasting Time – 7 – 6

Verse 3:
I ain't no rough guy, ain't no tough guy.
Don't get out much, and don't dress up fly.
A pawn in the game, that's all I am.
Givin' all my duckets to Uncle Sam, f*** it.
I'm free to do what I please, little lady.
I was born at night but not last night, baby.
I've been around, seen some things.
I've slept in dumpsters, got high with kings.
I don't bring much, ain't got a lot to say
But I got more time than Morris Day.
Puffin' a Winston, drinkin' a 4-0,
Kid Rock and I'm-a let you know.
(To Chorus:)

WEAPON & THE WOUND

Words and Music by
TRAVIS MEEKS

*Two gtrs. arr. for one.

Weapon & the Wound - 12 - 1

386

Weapon & the Wound - 12 - 5

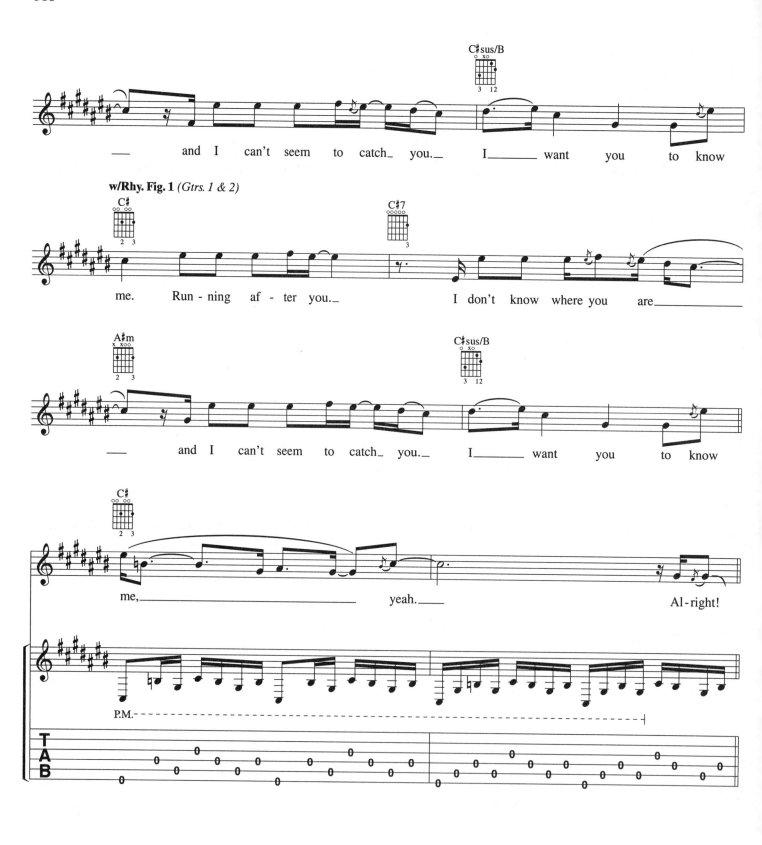

Reed Solo:

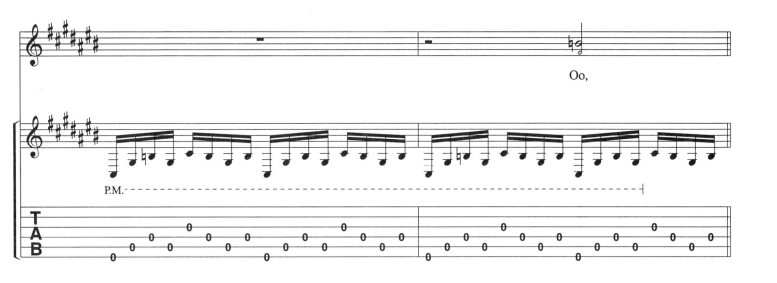

Oo,

Bridge:

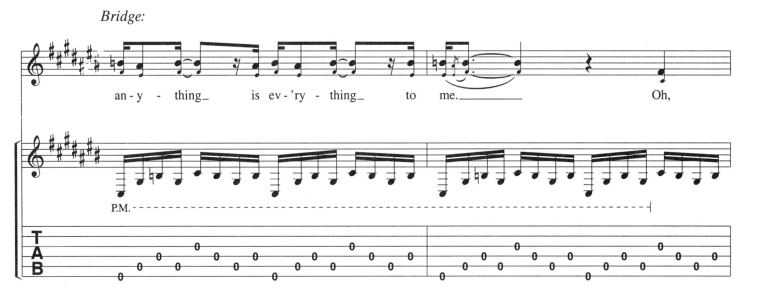

an-y-thing____ is ev-'ry-thing____ to me._____ Oh,

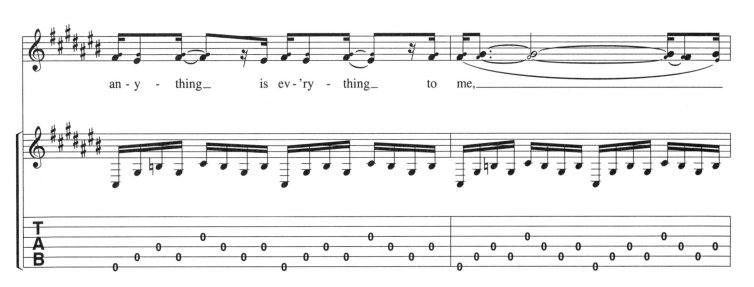

an-y-thing____ is ev-'ry-thing____ to me,_____

390

Don't know where you are.____ I_____ want you to know

me.

Outro:

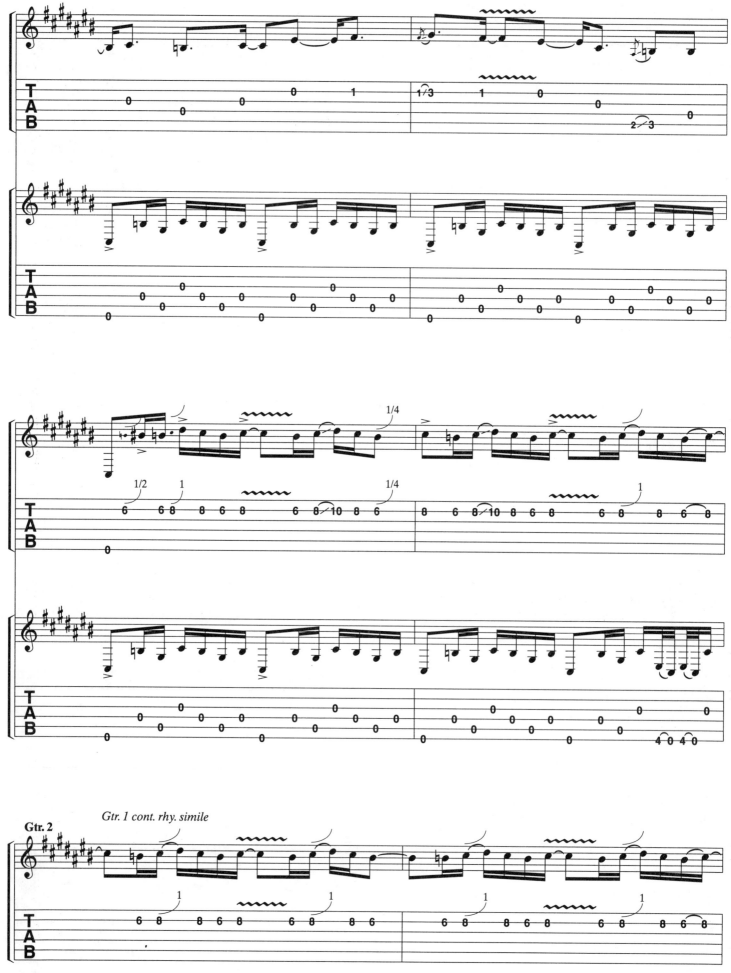

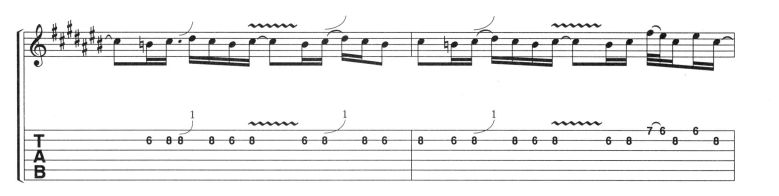

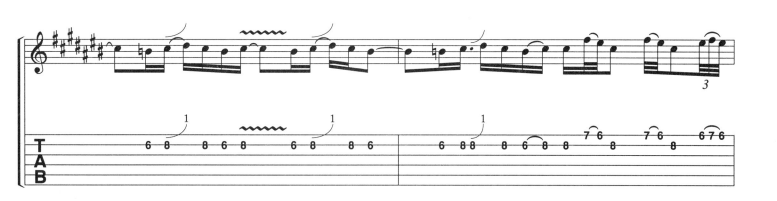

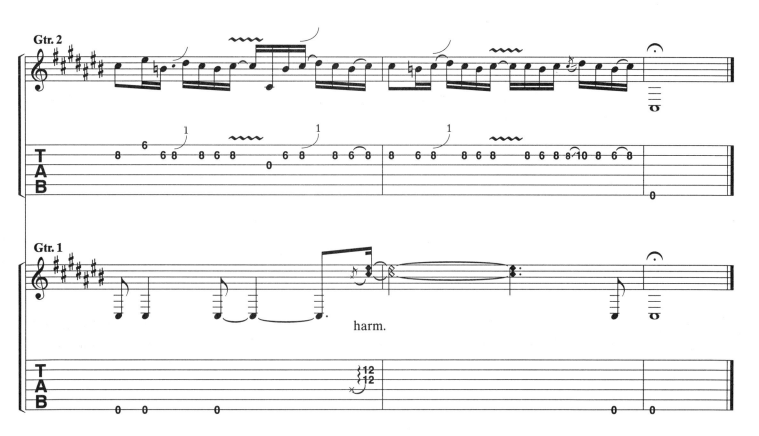

harm.

YOU'RE A GOD

Words and Music by
MATTHEW SCANELL

*Verses 2 & 3 only.

You're a God - 4 - 1

396

*Elec. Gtr. 2
Rhy. Fig. 1

Chorus:

you're a god___ and I am not.___ And I just thought. that

* 2 gtrs. arr. for 1 throughout section.

w/Rhy. Fig. 1 *(Elec. Gtr. 2)*

end Rhy. Fig. 1

you would know._____ You're a god___ and I am not.___ And

To Coda

Elec. Gtr. 2

I just thought_ I'd let you go.___

2.

Guitar Solo:

Elec. Gtr. 2

let you go.___

Elec. Gtr. 1

You're a God - 4 - 3

You're a God - 4 - 4

GUITAR TAB GLOSSARY **

TABLATURE EXPLANATION

READING TABLATURE: Tablature illustrates the six strings of the guitar. Notes and chords are indicated by the placement of fret numbers on a given string(s).

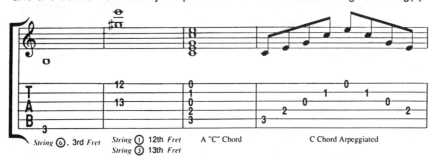

String ⑥, 3rd Fret   String ① 12th Fret   A "C" Chord   C Chord Arpeggiated
                       String ③ 13th Fret

BENDING NOTES

HALF STEP: Play the note and bend string one half step.*

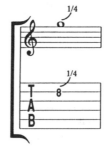

SLIGHT BEND (Microtone): Play the note and bend string slightly to the equivalent of half a fret.

BEND AND RELEASE: Play the note and gradually bend to the next pitch, then release to the original note. Only the first note is attacked.

WHOLE STEP: Play the note and bend string one whole step.

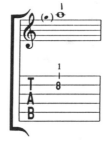

PREBEND (Ghost Bend): Bend to the specified note, before the string is picked.

BENDS INVOLVING MORE THAN ONE STRING: Play the note and bend string while playing an additional note (or notes) on another string(s). Upon release, relieve pressure from additional note(s), causing original note to sound alone.

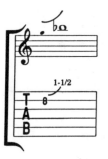

WHOLE STEP AND A HALF: Play the note and bend string a whole step and a half.

PREBEND AND RELEASE: Bend the string, play it, then release to the original note.

BENDS INVOLVING STATIONARY NOTES: Play notes and bend lower pitch, then hold until release begins (indicated at the point where line becomes solid).

UNISON BEND: Play both notes and immediately bend the lower note to the same pitch as the higher note.

TWO STEPS: Play the note and bend string two whole steps.

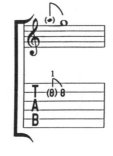

REVERSE BEND: Play the already-bent string, then immediately drop it down to the fretted note.

DOUBLE NOTE BEND: Play both notes and immediately bend both strings simultaneously.

*A half step is the smallest interval in Western music; it is equal to one fret. A whole step equals two frets.

© 1990 Beam Me Up Music
c/o CPP/Belwin, Inc. Miami, Florida 33014
International Copyright Secured   Made in U.S.A.   All Rights Reserved   **By Kenn Chipkin and Aaron Stang

RHYTHM SLASHES

STRUM INDICA-TIONS: Strum with indicated rhythm.

The chord voicings are found on the first page of the transcription underneath the song title.

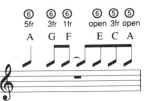

INDICATING SINGLE NOTES USING RHYTHM SLASHES: Very often single notes are incorporated into a rhythm part. The note name is indicated above the rhythm slash with a fret number and a string indication.

ARTICULATIONS

HAMMER ON: Play lower note, then "hammer on" to higher note with another finger. Only the first note is attacked.

LEFT HAND HAMMER: Hammer on the first note played on each string with the left hand.

PULL OFF: Play higher note, then "pull off" to lower note with another finger. Only the first note is attacked.

FRET-BOARD TAPPING: "Tap" onto the note indicated by + with a finger of the pick hand, then pull off to the following note held by the fret hand.

TAP SLIDE: Same as fretboard tapping, but the tapped note is slid randomly up the fretboard, then pulled off to the following note.

BEND AND TAP TECHNIQUE: Play note and bend to specified interval. While holding bend, tap onto note indicated.

LEGATO SLIDE: Play note and slide to the following note. (Only first note is attacked).

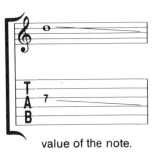

LONG GLISSAN-DO: Play note and slide in specified direction for the full value of the note.

SHORT GLISSAN-DO: Play note for its full value and slide in specified direction at the last possible moment.

PICK SLIDE: Slide the edge of the pick in specified direction across the length of the string(s).

MUTED STRINGS: A percussive sound is made by laying the fret hand across all six strings while pick hand strikes specified area (low, mid, high strings).

PALM MUTE: The note or notes are muted by the palm of the pick hand by lightly touching the string(s) near the bridge.

TREMOLO PICKING: The note or notes are picked as fast as possible.

TRILL: Hammer on and pull off consecutively and as fast as possible between the original note and the grace note.

ACCENT: Notes or chords are to be played with added emphasis.

STACCATO (Detached Notes): Notes or chords are to be played roughly half their actual value and with separation.

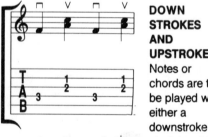

DOWN STROKES AND UPSTROKES: Notes or chords are to be played with either a downstroke (⊓ ·) or upstroke (∨) of the pick.

VIBRATO: The pitch of a note is varied by a rapid shaking of the fret hand finger, wrist, and forearm.

HARMONICS

NATURAL HARMONIC: A finger of the fret hand lightly touches the note or notes indicated in the tab and is played by the pick hand.

ARTIFICIAL HARMONIC: The first tab number is fretted, then the pick hand produces the harmonic by using a finger to lightly touch the same string at the second tab number (in parenthesis) and is then picked by another finger.

ARTIFICIAL "PINCH" HARMONIC: A note is fretted as indicated by the tab, then the pick hand produces the harmonic by squeezing the pick firmly while using the tip of the index finger in the pick attack. If parenthesis are found around the fretted note, it does not sound. No parenthesis means both the fretted note and A.H. are heard simultaneously.

TREMOLO BAR

SPECIFIED INTERVAL: The pitch of a note or chord is lowered to a specified interval and then may or may not return to the original pitch. The activity of the tremolo bar is graphically represented by peaks and valleys.

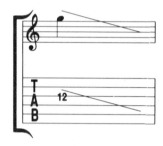

UN-SPECIFIED INTERVAL: The pitch of a note or a chord is lowered to an unspecified interval.